ITALIAN
VEGETARIAN COOKING

ITALIAN VEGETARIAN COOKING

EMANUELA STUCCHI

FOREWORD BY LORENZA DE'MEDICI

PHOTOGRAPHS BY GUS FILGATE

PAVILION

This edition published in Great Britain
in 1996 by Pavilion Books Limited
London House
Great Eastern Wharf
Parkgate Road
London SW11 4NQ

A CIP catalogue record for this book is
available from the
British Library

ISBN 1-85793-830 5
D.L.B.: 3.373-1998

Printed and bound in Spain
by Egedsa

10 9 8 7 6 5 4 3 2

This book may be ordered by post direct
from the publisher.
Please contact the Marketing Department.
But try your bookshop first.

Contents

Foreword

Ever since I was a child, I always had the opportunity to eat very well. Our family cook was famous throughout Milan for her splendid and elaborate dinners. Flaky pastries were always made at home, as were pâtés, vegetable terrines and other baked treats. Our everyday food was just as carefully prepared: light and appetizing, according to the desire of my father, a passionate gourmet who would always bring home recipes which my mother would faithfully transcribe into a notebook.

All through my youth my palate was encouraged to develop, and when I got married I brought this heritage into my family. Meanwhile great cooks became a disappearing race and the heads of families began to familiarize themselves with the pleasures and secrets of the kitchen, having to take charge of things personally. And so I did too, and in the best tradition my children began very early in life to educate their palates, stimulated by good cooking, taking on this heritage in their turn.

To cook well is a gift, but expressing this is more still, as the pleasure of sharing grows with many more people. My daughter, Emanuela, not only has the gift of cooking well, she also has the gift of being able to communicate it on paper, creating recipes that invite others to share in her competence and creativity. I am particularly proud that my inheritance is in such good hands. And as times change and cooking evolves along with them, in this book Emanuela has specifically dedicated herself to the art of vegetarian cooking. Fruits and vegetables, cereals, and dried beans and peas have always been a grand passion with her, so she has been comfortable creating this book, principally dedicated to light and healthy cooking.

Like all young people, she has enjoyed travelling a great deal, especially in the last few years since she has taken charge of the family farm, Badia a Coltibuono, in Tuscany. In her role as ambassador for Italian cooking and wines, Emanuela has had the opportunity to explore new styles and trends of cuisine, always keeping Italian cooking as her main point of reference. I believe few peoples are as passionately fond of their own cooking as the Italians – for the excellent reason that it is so healthy.

LORENZA DE' MEDICI, 1994

Introduction

For those of us privileged to live in the beautiful Tuscan countryside, it is very simple to go downstairs to the vegetable garden and be inspired by the selection of ripe produce available, to create the menu of the day. Our vegetable garden is found right in the middle of the main garden, like a jewel in a setting of flowers.

My mother adores gardening and has returned from her world travels with cuttings or seeds from all manner of interesting herbs and salad greens. Exposed to this abundance, we have all learned that the secret of successful cooking lies in choosing fresh ingredients and allowing their flavours to speak for themselves.

The great majority of the recipes in this book are firmly rooted in Italy's traditional family cuisine. The others, perhaps a little more modern, are still bound up with the past, the historic use of vegetables, rice, pasta, extra virgin olive oil and fruit. Don't be afraid if you're not yet an expert cook – none of these recipes is particularly difficult. In the introductions to the chapters and recipes I've suggested some tips to help you create new and interesting variations on basic themes, often with the judicious use of herbs. The most crucial point to consider when adding and changing seasonings is not to overpower the palate with an over-complex mixture of flavours.

The real secret of Italian cooking is simplicity. Ingredients demand the utmost respect for their natural flavour and texture, and should never be covered up with too many elements or sauces. Fruits and vegetables invariably taste better if they are ripened in the sunshine and are as fresh from the soil as possible. And produce in season that is grown locally is always preferable to that imported from a distance. Ideally, buy direct from a farmer who grows organically, using natural methods to combat weeds and pests. Vegetables and fruit grown in this way are undoubtedly more delicious. Of course, not everyone has access to vegetables of this quality. And organic produce costs considerably more than vegetables grown by modern farming methods. Fortunately, more and more farmers are adopting methods of cultivation that, while significantly more labour-intensive, produce better quality produce with a positive effect on the earth from which they came.

THE ESSENTIAL ITALIAN
vegetables

Italy has a temperate climate with four clearly defined seasons. Its rich soil provides an almost infinite choice of vegetables, and this abundance has of course influenced our dietary habits. Up until after the Second World War Italy's economy was mainly rural and relatively undeveloped; meat was a rarity, and for this reason a mainly vegetarian cuisine evolved spontaneously. It still thrives to this day, although meat is now eaten daily by most people.

Vegetables are among the best sources of vitamins, minerals and fibre that we have. (Fibre, by the way, is a great blessing for those who are trying to lose weight, as it gives satisfaction with fewer calories.) This is why the Mediterranean diet is growing in popularity at a tremendous rate, as more and more people realize its health advantages, not to mention its delicious flavours. Between salads, soups, purées, stews and simple cooked dishes, there is a great wealth of choice for vegetable recipes to make up interesting menus.

The most important factor in choosing vegetables is knowing the season during which they grow. In general, the signs of good quality produce are freshness, ripeness and a firm, solid consistency. Many vegetables do not need to be refrigerated: a cool and airy place will be fine for their storage.

artichoke

aubergine (eggplant)

beans

broccoli

Brussels sprouts

cabbage

cardoon

carrot

cauliflower

celery

cucumber

fennel

garlic

leek

mushrooms

onion

pepper

potato

salad leaves

spinach

squashes

Swiss chard

tomato

turnips

Artichoke

CARCIOFO

This particular vegetable contains many nutrients, such as sodium, potassium and vitamin C as well as fibre. Its slightly bitter taste is a clue to its curative powers – it is well known for its hepatic, or liver-healing, properties. Globe artichokes are delicious raw or cooked. For serving them raw, choose small ones with a long shape; the larger, rounder ones are better cooked. The best specimens have tightly closed leaves and feel solid. Unless very small artichokes are used, it is necessary to remove the hairy choke from the centre.

Do this before or after cooking.

Raw artichokes are eaten with olive oil and salt, or sliced with Parmesan flakes in a salad. Both of these make wonderful first courses. Cooked artichokes may be served whole, or just the fleshy bottom is used. Artichokes discolour quickly once cut so to avoid this unaesthetic inconvenience simply squeeze a few drops of lemon juice into some water and bathe the prepared artichokes, keeping them immersed until you need them.

Aubergine (Eggplant)

MELANZANA

Like tomatoes and potatoes, the aubergine (eggplant) is a member of the Solanacae or nightshade family. It is rich in folic acid and potassium.

In southern Italy, the aubergine (eggplant) is nicknamed 'poor man's meat' and it is this almost meaty texture that makes it so valuable in vegetarian dishes. Braised or grilled, aubergines (eggplants) also make a delicious low-calorie addition to rice and pasta dishes.

To make aubergines (eggplants) more digestible, slice and sprinkle with coarse salt, then leave to sweat out their bitterish juice for about an hour, although this isn't necessary for young aubergines (eggplants). When you are ready to cook them, pat them dry with paper towels. It is advisable to cut aubergines (eggplants) just before use, as they blacken rapidly on contact with the air.

Broad Beans (Fava Beans), Green Beans and Peas

FAVE, FAGIOLINI E PISELLI

In Italy broad beans (fava beans) are mainly eaten raw, and this is why their appearance is the sign that spring has arrived: they are plentiful on local market stalls at this time of the year. This is also the time of year that fresh pecorino cheese is available – due to the lambing the ewes have an abundance of milk. The combination of young broad beans (fava beans) and fresh pecorino is about as irresistible as ripe cherries. One mouthful has an uncanny way of leading to the next.

In common with all beans, broad beans (fava beans) are a good source of B vitamins and fibre.

Practically calorie-free, green beans contain abundant fibre as well as lots of vitamin A and potassium. Absolutely delicious, they are often eaten, steamed and cooled, in summer salads with other raw vegetables. They are also combined with boiled potatoes. They keep well in the refrigerator if left a little damp after washing them: put them in a bowl and cover them with a dampened paper towel. They are very quick to cook, either steamed or boiled. To keep their crunchy texture and brilliant green colour, run cold water over them immediately after draining. They are irresistible served with Green Sauce (see page 155).

Peas, especially fresh ones, are very popular in Italy: their sweetness makes them a favourite accompaniment to many dishes. They can also be found in a classic rice soup, mixed with pasta and béchamel sauce and baked in the oven, in vegetable terrines and many more dishes.

The most prized peas are those picked young, when they are still very sweet and not floury. They can be cooked in very little water, and then added to fried

onions, for example. A pinch of sugar along with a pinch of salt will help accentuate their sweetness and make them even more tasty. A herb that blends particularly well with peas is tarragon.

Peas lose little flavour in the freezing process, and they are always handy to have in the freezer for an emergency. Their composition is exceptionally balanced – high in fibre, protein and vitamin A, very low in fat – so it's advisable to make plentiful use of them in the diet.

Broccoli, Cauliflower and Brussels Sprouts
BROCCOLI, CAVOLFIORE E CAVOLINI

All members of the Brassica family, these vegetables offer high calcium, vitamin C and carotene content together with the absolute absence of fat.

Popular broccoli is easily obtainable and is delicious in many recipes. Summer is its season. In the market, look for tight, compact heads of unopened flowers (florets), firm stalks and a dark rich green colour. Cooking broccoli is very simple. One delicious way, much enjoyed in Puglia, is to add florets to a pan of pasta, with a little oil and salt, and to cook them all together. Drain and dress with extra virgin olive oil seasoned with a little garlic and chilli pepper. Serve with freshly grated pecorino cheese.

Cauliflower is also very popular in Italian cooking, principally enjoyed in winter. It is useful both for first courses and robust main dishes.

Looking like miniature cabbages, Brussels sprouts are delicious both raw (shredded in salads) and cooked. But they must never be overcooked or they will be most unpleasant.

A secret to help prevent the sometimes strong cooking smell of the Brassica family is to add a little vinegar to the boiling water. Cut a deep cross in the base of the stalks to ensure that they will cook in the same time as the florets or heads.

Cabbage
CAVOLO

Hiding in the leaves of dark cabbage is a rich supply of precious vitamins and minerals such as iron, zinc and sulphur, the last of which is all too evident in its cooking aroma. One way to reduce the cooking smell is to add a stalk of celery while boiling.

Cabbage is eaten in many ways all over Italy. White cabbage is sliced very thinly and eaten as salad (see page 62). Then there's red cabbage, which is good both raw and cooked in soups. The so-called black cabbage is the number one ingredient of the best and tastiest soup. Or, boil the long leaves in lightly salted water, drain and serve in soup plates on top of bread slices that have been rubbed with a garlic clove.

Cardoon and Celery
CARDI E SEDANO

The cardoon, which looks like a large bunch of flat celery, is in season mid-winter to early spring. The long, silvery-green stalks need at least half an hour's boiling to become tender. After boiling they are useful in many recipes, where their slight bitterness enhances the dish. One delicious way to prepare them is to bake them in the oven, cut into little pieces, as if they were potatoes. They must be baked for a long time, right up to the point where they are almost burned. Another tasty way is to cover them, once boiled, with béchamel sauce and bake them in the oven.

Cardoons are rich in potassium, calcium and iron.

Celery is one of the key ingredients in *soffritto*, the heart of innumerable traditional Italian dishes, such as soups, sauces and minestrones. Celery sticks can also be dipped into a soft cheese or bean purée. Together with fennel, carrots and spring onions (scallions), celery sticks are part of *pinzimonio*, a traditional appetizer where the vegetables are dipped in extra virgin olive oil and salt.

Carrot
CAROTE

This vegetable is a little goldmine of carotene from which we produce vitamin A – a vitamin noted for its wonderful effects on the skin. Interestingly, carotene becomes more concentrated when carrots are cooked. The high fibre content of this vegetable makes it a satisfying and healthy raw snack. The slight sweetness of carrots appeals to children, thereby reducing a craving for sugary treats.

Organically grown carrots have a particularly fine flavour. With young organic carrots you can even make a light salad from the tender leaves. Choose carrots that are dark orange and firm. They are delicious raw, just grated or sliced very thinly and left to marinate in extra virgin olive oil and lemon juice.

Cucumber
CETRIOLO

Extremely refreshing, cucumber blends beautifully with salad leaves. As an appetizer, cucumber can be sliced and simply dressed with dill, lemon juice and extra virgin olive oil. Another very tasty way, inspired by the Greeks, is to dress slices or cubes with oil, plain yogurt, garlic slices and a few mint leaves. Cucumber soup is a delicately flavoured first course. To make it, just simmer chopped cucumber with a few pieces of potato covered with half water and half milk; purée and season with a little white wine before serving. Cucumber juice is a good tonic astringent for the skin.

Fennel
FINOCCHIO

This vegetable is precious to the vegetarian cook because it has enough flavour to stand alone as the basis of a robust dish.

A classic risotto made with fennel, sliced and browned with the onions, is a wonderful main course; a few fennel seeds added towards the end will contribute an intriguing complexity.

Fennel is high in fibre and very low in calories.

Garlic
AGLIO

Garlic is famous for its health-giving properties. It has been scientifically proven to inhibit the growth of many bacteria, though I understand you need to eat about ten to twelve cloves a day for this benefit! Garlic contains vitamin C so it's useful if you feel a cold coming on. Studies have also shown the benefits of garlic to patients with heart disease.

Some people find the smell of garlic on the breath to be objectionable, although if you eat garlic regularly, you'll find this reaction diminishes. If you're worried, chewing a little fresh parsley or some coffee beans will do the trick of neutralizing the aroma. Still, best not eat it before going to a concert!

In the kitchen garlic is a king: its perfume while frying makes the appetite perk up, and its flavour is essential to so many soups, stews and sauces for pasta. Raw garlic is used in many sauces. For those who find it a bit indigestible like this, here's a handy tip: instead of adding it to the sauce, rub the serving dish with a peeled clove. This will give you the perfume with no difficulties for the digestion.

Leek
PORRI

Leeks have plenty of nutritional value and are wonderfully tasty. They have a gentle flavour, somewhat
sweeter than a spring onion (scallion) and much easier
to digest. The tender inner parts can be eaten raw.

Cooked leeks are delicious, especially with eggs. Try
substituting them for Swiss chard in the pie on page
92. They should be parboiled first, then bound with
egg and ricotta. Leeks are also good steamed and then
dressed with extra virgin olive oil and lemon juice.

Mushrooms
FUNGHI

Wild mushrooms are a great gift from nature, present-
ing us with all their intense earthy flavours. The
adventure of hunting them is only advisable with a
reliable guide who is knowledgeable, as one mistake
can prove to be serious. For most people fresh wild
mushrooms are a rare treat due to the high prices.

The first rule with wild mushrooms is to inspect
them carefully, from stalk to cap, as many wild animals are greedy for them and sometimes their bites
allow worms to enter and eat out the insides too. Take
care then to select the mushrooms one by one.

Wild mushrooms need no washing; just wipe them
gently with a towel and peel or trim them with a sharp
knife wherever they are bruised. Cook them rapidly,
with few other flavours – a dab of garlic, a little extra
virgin olive oil. Fry them with a little butter and
lemon juice or cook under the grill (broiler) with rosemary and parsley. If they are not the best of quality,

stew them with onions, butter, rosemary and a little bay leaf. A good home-made pasta deserves to be dressed with porcini mushrooms, simply sliced and fried with butter, salt and pepper. The flavours are so rich and complex that nothing more is needed.

Dried mushrooms can be very useful for stews and stuffings. They need only be soaked in warm water for about 20 minutes. Strain the water carefully, as it will have little bits of grit in it. This water will make an excellent base for soups and sauces. Fresh cultivated mushrooms are a good alternative when wild ones are unavailable. Cooking times will be shorter because they are less substantial than their wild counterparts. Cultivated common mushrooms can be braised with white wine, puréed and added to sauces and seasonings to enhance them. Cultivated mushrooms have much less flavour than their wild counterparts, so it's a good idea to add herbs and spices to make them more interesting. Garlic, thyme, oregano and mint work well, to name but a few.

Onion
CIPOLLA

The humble onion is the base of almost every savoury dish. It can also be boiled, steamed, fried, braised or baked. It's a great addition to pizza and pasta. Spring onions (scallions) are young tender onions, often added to salads. When at the market, choose good-looking onions that are firm. They should not have green shoots coming out of the tops. The onion is a healthy vegetable, aiding many functions of the body.

Pepper
PEPERONI

Red, yellow, orange or green, sweet peppers are extremely versatile and tasty. Their happy colours will cheer up salads, both raw and cooked, as well as pasta or rice dishes and soups. They are also fantastic stuffed, raw or cooked. One of the best ways to eat them is baked, drizzled with extra virgin olive oil, seasoned with garlic and parsley, and served with bruschetta (see page 54). On the slim chance that you don't eat them all up at once, keep them in the refrigerator – their flavour will improve over the next few days. You can substitute sweet peppers for tomatoes in the recipe on page 88, remembering to moisten the rice stuffing often with a little vegetable stock.

One of the most wonderful things about sweet peppers is their vitamin C content – each pepper has as much of this precious vitamin as two oranges.

Potato
PATATE

Here's a vegetable that's coming in for some re-evaluation. Full of fibre and nutrients, the potato makes a valuable contribution to a well-balanced vegetarian diet. Fried potatoes are delicious, but don't eat them too often because they can absorb a lot of oil. (For this reason, it's important to use a good quality oil – ideally extra virgin olive oil). Boiling leaches away a lot of the potatoes' nutrients, so it's preferable to steam them.

When preparing potatoes, throw away any that are green-tinged or sprouting. Also, cut them just before cooking because they can discolour.

Salad Leaves
INSALATE

Salad is a daily habit here in Italy, made either with lettuce in one of its many varieties, or any of the many other greens available, such as chicory (Belgian endive), radicchio, frisé (curly endive), watercress and rocket (arugula). It's worth noting that the rich supply of iron in red radicchio is even more easily assimilated by the body than that found in spinach.

It's a good idea to serve a salad at every main meal, to keep the balance between cooked and raw vegetables. Choose unwilted leaves that are tender and tasty, and wash them thoroughly but rapidly – all the vitamins tend to disappear into the water if left soaking.

Spinach
SPINACI

One of the most important members of the family of leafy greens, spinach is much loved for its strikingly mineral taste. This vegetable is particularly rich in vitamin C. Although spinach is rich in iron, only two to five percent is available to the body because of the oxalic acid in spinach.

Spinach is excellent raw. For this use choose only the little tender leaves at the centre of the plant, and enjoy them mixed with a variety of other vegetables, as they add a contrasting spicy note. To cook spinach, wash the leaves very carefully in plenty of water, shake them a little and place them in a covered saucepan – there is no need to add any water as their own will be quite sufficient. When tender, drain well and then sauté in a little butter. Finally, add a sprinkling of Parmesan and a pinch of grated nutmeg. This is the classic accompaniment that with mashed potatoes appears at the side of many main course dishes.

Squashes
ZUCCA

These are versatile garden vegetables full of fibre. Summer squashes with edible skins – courgettes (zucchini) and pattyian, for example – also provide vitamin C, while hard-shelled winter squashes (pumpkin, butternut, etc) provide vitamin A; all squashes contain potassium.

The warm orange colour of squashes such as pumpkin is pretty in soups and risottos. These vegetables also make a delicious purée, to which you can give a spicy touch with some curry powder. In the Padana plains, around the banks of the River Po in north Italy, the local tradition is to use pumpkin for the most delicious tortelli stuffing imaginable. If you're ever travelling in the area, it is worth dropping in to a restaurant and asking for this speciality. It is made so well – nowhere else is it so velvety and sweet.

Courgettes (zucchini) are a very popular member of the squash family, and have the advantage of being versatile and easy to grow. Baby courgettes (zucchini) are a gourmet's dream: delicious when eaten raw, I suggest you serve them simply grated and dressed with a little extra virgin olive oil, lemon juice and mint. Courgette (zucchini) flowers are also highly esteemed and used frequently in Italian cooking: they liven up salads with their joyful colour, and add to the flavour of a *soffritto* in a tomato sauce.

Swiss Chard
BIETOLE

These big green leaves have as much nourishment as one could ever ask from one vegetable. They belong to the same family of leafy greens as beetroot and spinach, as well as many wild vegetables, picked in spring in the fields and meadows. High in vitamins A and C and iron, they have the added advantage of being packed with protein. At the market look for produce of intense green and avoid limp, wilted leaves. Swiss chard is in season almost all the year round, but if you'd like to make sure of your supply, it freezes very well.

Cooking Swiss chard is a breeze – simply steam or drop into a little boiling water for a few minutes cooking. Dress with a little extra virgin olive oil and lemon juice. This way the subtle flavours will only be enhanced, not disguised. Another tasty way to prepare them is to sauté them in oil with a little garlic and chilli pepper.

Tomato

POMODORO

Tomatoes are the queen in the Italian kitchen – the foundation for sauces, soups and countless other dishes. Generally speaking, round tomatoes are better for eating raw – the best are thin-skinned, have few seeds and a bright red colour. The plum- or pear-shaped tomatoes, are traditionally used in sauces.

Tomatoes are very good for you, containing vitamins A, B and C and minerals (potassium, iron and phosphorus), and when ripe they taste wonderful. It is not necessary to store tomatoes in the refrigerator.

For those fortunate enough to have their own vegetable garden, plum tomatoes freeze very well, for use in the winter. Just wash them and freeze them as they are, with a sprig of basil. When you want to cook them, run them under hot water; in a few seconds their skins will peel off. Put them in a saucepan and let them thaw over a low heat. When they are soft add a *soffritto* (see page 156) and you will have a delicious sauce in next to no time.

Turnips

RAPE

Surprisingly enough, turnips are a member of the cabbage family. They are considered a modest vegetable, but those who love them appreciate their sweetness, with a little hint of something earthy and spicy in the background. Look for small or medium-sized ones at the market – big turnips will be too fibrous and will have a strong taste. The smaller ones don't even need to be peeled.

Turnips are used in minestrone, and they are also delicious steamed or sautéed. The baby ones are very good raw in salads. Dress them with a mixture of olive oil and lemon juice, in which a few crushed juniper berries have been infused for a while. Turnips contain a moderate amount of vitamin C.

THE ESSENTIAL ITALIAN *fruits*

In the classical scheme of the Italian meal, fruit is the final dish. But now that we are finding out more about the digestive process this is changing. It has been discovered that fruit digests better if it passes rapidly through the system without being long delayed in the stomach. The enzymes necessary for good digestion of fruit exist when the stomach is empty; eaten at the end of the meal it interferes with the breakdown of starches and the result is a swollen feeling, caused by fementation. Once cooked, however, fruit becomes easily assimilated, so the whole argument changes. But the calorie content can mount significantly when fruit is cooked in a dessert – substituting honey for sugar in the recipes makes a tasty alternative, although sadly no less fattening!

Italian cuisine includes a wide variety of fruit tarts, pies and cakes, and is famous for its fruit sorbets and ice creams. Another way to enjoy the summer's harvest of fruits is to preserve them. Making jams, jellies and other preserves at home lets you decide how much and what kind of sweetener is used and you can ensure that the quality of the fruit is the best. Walnuts, hazelnuts, chestnuts, almonds and pine nuts are also grown extensively all over the Italian peninsula. We use them with passion, since their flavours and distinctive crunchy texture add the perfect note of surprise to any dish.

apple

apricot

banana

berries and cherries

chestnut

citrus fruits

figs

melon

pear

plum

strawberries

Apple
MELA

Common wisdom used to hold that apples are filling, but research now shows that they actually have a stimulating effect on the digestive juices. There are many different varieties of apples on the market, and most people already have their favourite ways of preparing them. The floury types are much better for cooking, stuffings and apple sauce. The ones with a finer-grained flesh are better for eating raw and in fruit salads. After slicing them, always remember to sprinkle with a little lemon juice, as this will stop them oxidizing and turning an unappetizing brown.

Apricot
ALBICOCCA

The apricot tree has a peculiar habit of producing bumper harvests every three years or so. Instead of letting this glut go to waste, in Italy a most delicious jam is made.

Apricots have many outstanding nutritional benefits, making them a precious addition to a varied diet. They are a good source of vitamin A, which can be detected by their vivid yellow-orange colour, a sure sign of high levels of carotene. They also contain significant doses of vitamin C, potassium and iron.

Dried apricots make a deliciously chewy snack – richer in nutrients and fibre than fresh apricots – though you should always keep in mind that the sugar content in dried fruit is four to five times as high as that in fresh fruit. Canned apricots are usually sweetened far too much.

Banana
BANANA

Bananas do not refrigerate well, yet they are one of the few fruits that ripen to satisfaction after harvesting. They are extremely high in potassium, and in pregnancy can help counteract the leg cramps that often occur due to a lack of this mineral. They also have a high vitamin and fibre content.

Bananas are delicious in fruit salads, play a part in many desserts, and make a healthy snack for children. Try them whipped with honey and yogurt in the blender.

Berries and Cherries
FRUTTI DI BOSCO E CILIEGIE

Even though you might find it hard to believe, berries are full of fibre. And they contain lots of vitamin C – strawberries have as much of this vitamin as the same weight of oranges.

The wealth of different berry flavours will inspire many ways to use them in cakes, tarts, fruit salads, ice creams and puddings. Berries need to be kept refrigerated and not washed too much (they can become soggy). If they need washing it's better to do it at the last minute, and pat them dry afterwards. I like to dip strawberries in white wine and roll them in sugar. Most berries freeze very well. Made into a purée, they make a nice treat in the winter.

'One leads to another,' is what is said about cherries – when they're good they are irresistible, especially the dark, almost black ones with the rich, sweet flesh. When choosing cherries, take care to avoid any blemished ones, as they will spoil the others if placed together.

Cherries are very seasonal, and their arrival creates a summer mood immediately. They are delicious both raw and cooked, making luscious jams and preserves, topping for ice cream, and tart filling. Try mashing them with a little sugar, leaving overnight and then baking for a delicious dessert. Freshly made cherry juice is truly out of this world.

Chestnuts
CASTAGNE

In Italy chestnuts are popular prepared in many different ways. The best-known recipe is White Mountain (see page 138), a dessert much loved by children. These days it is rarer, as much patience and work is needed for the peeling of the chestnuts. Sometimes you find a version of this dessert in the pastry shop, which uses chestnut jam; however, once you have had the real thing, these imitations will not do. A quintessentially simple dessert, it is an absolute must to try. Castagnaccio (see page 140) is another delicious recipe, this time from Tuscany. Chestnuts are also used for stuffings, and added to soups.

All nuts are high in carbohydrates, fibre and protein, although to make this protein 'complete' (and thus useful to the body), the nuts should be eaten with beans when forming the main part of a meal.

Citrus Fruits
LIMONI E ARANCE

There is no need to praise the health benefits of citrus any further: their reputation as providers of vitamin C in particular is already deservedly widespread.

Lemons serve in so many ways in Italian cooking. One of their more useful properties is that of inhibiting oxidation: a few drops will stop apples, bananas, artichokes and so on from discolouring when left exposed to the air. Mixed with extra virgin olive oil, lemon juice makes an alternative to vinegar in a salad dressing – this is particularly suitable for bitter salad leaves such as radicchio or spinach. It is also ideal with *la mesticanza*, a collection of wild greens much appre-

Figs
FICHI

The very beautiful fig tree fills the air with its unmistakable perfume in the summertime. The fruit is eaten very ripe, often with Parma ham, although it is wonderful with fresh goats' cheese. Ricotta is another alternative, for dessert. Fig jam is a classic, especially if you don't like your jams too sweet – the figs are cooked with green lemons.

Figs, both fresh and dried, are a good source of carbohydrates, fibre, iron, calcium and potassium.

ciated in Rome. Old ladies can be seen harvesting the greens in the fields at the periphery of the city, and carrying them for sale to the Campo dei fiori market.

In Sicily there are many dishes that employ citrus fruit because there are vast fruit groves in that area. Lemon is sliced very thin to be served with fennel. Oranges may be used as a starter or even as a side dish, dressed with extra virgin olive oil, salt and olives.

Melon
MELONE

Among the many varieties of melons there are some that last until the first cold snap of winter, while others are only found in summertime. Melons contain fibre, as well as vitamins A and C and potassium. They are pleasantly refreshing, and have a diuretic effect on the body. They are used in first courses and for desserts, often filled with fruit salad.

When choosing melon in the market, look for vine-ripened fruit (the scar at the stalk end should be clean and sunken) – these melons will be sweet with an intense fragrance.

Pear
PERE

The pear is a fruit of subtle flavour; if it is not allowed to ripen on the tree it will be bland and tasteless. Although it's true that being so sweet, pears spoil easily, it's still just not worth buying unripe produce. It's better to buy a few at a time, as you need them. The best have brightly coloured, thin skin and fine-grained flesh.

In Tuscany pears are traditionally eaten with aged pecorino cheese. Pears are also delicious combined with chocolate, so try stewing pears and serve with chocolate cake (see page 143)

Pears are a moderate source of fibre, and contain potassium and some vitamin C (mainly in the skin).

Plum
SUSINE

Plums grown on a large scale are a far cry from the small and tasty country plums. If you grow your own fruit you will appreciate the difference. Fresh plums contain vitamins A, B and C as well as fibre, but their chief benefit is their gentle, but powerful laxative effect once dried. Prunes (dried plums) have more fibre than dried beans, and the vitamin content is much increased in this concentrated form. Prunes are also a rich source of potassium.

Fresh plums are good stewed (serve them with ice cream), and they make a particularly fine jam.

Strawberries
FRAGOLE

Strawberries are one of nature's most wonderful inventions, with a distinctive perfume and a delicious taste which few other fruits can match. This beautifully coloured fruit has always had pride of place at the Italian table. Wild strawberries are particularly delicious, although some cultivated breeds are equally fragrant and tasty. Washing strawberries in water removes much of their flavour, so I recommend rinsing them in red wine, then serving them in a wine sauce sweetened with a little sugar. A squeeze of lemon juice will help to bring out the flavour.

THE VEGETARIAN
store
cupboard

The storecupboard is the heart of my kitchen. I am lucky enough to have a huge one: three large cupboard doors opening on to two spacious shelves where various culinary treasures are assembled. It is an inspiration to open a cupboard like this, brimming with every ingredient I could possibly use. Whether browsing in local shops or on foreign trips, I always give in to temptation and buy new or specialist products to store until I find just the right moment to try them out.

Behind the first two doors are packets of grains, dried vegetables, rices from around the world, pasta in various shapes, spices, dried herbs, and a collection of extra virgin olive oils. A very special corner is reserved for my collection of wines, which is not extensive but quite sufficient for everyday drinking. I always have a choice of whites and reds, simple wines suitable for everyday quaffing and more complex vintages for special occasions, rounded off with a few dessert wines and a couple of grappas.

The third cupboard encases a large fridge for the more perishable proteins. I also store fruit and vegetables here in the hot summer months, although it is preferable to avoid the fridge altogether and eat these as fresh as possible.

GRAINS

Cereals – barley, buckwheat, maize or corn, millet, rice and wheat – are very old friends to the human race, traced throughout history to the dawning of civilization. They are also some of our *best* friends – they are part of every meal we eat, from our breakfast roll to midnight snack. More cereals are grown, by a wide margin, than any other crop on earth.

The composition of cereals is very well balanced between protein, complex sugars, carbohydrates, minerals and important vitamins, if consumed in their whole and unpolished form, complete with valuable fibre.

There is great creativity in the use of cereal grains – different kinds of pasta, rice, spelt, buckwheat and so on. Legumes or pulses such as peas, beans and lentils also play very significant roles in our everyday diet, together with extra virgin olive oil.

Sprouting cereal grains adds much health giving nourishment: it transforms them, adding to their amino acids, protein and vitamins. Sprouts are little nutritional powerhouses, as well as being more digestible than when unsprouted.

GRAINS *Clockwise from left:* Whole wheat, oats, brown rice, risotto rice, barley (on spoons), millet, polenta

Barley
ORZO

Most people think of beer when barley is mentioned, but there are many other uses for this hardy cereal grain. In the Tuscan countryside ground roast barley is brewed to be drunk instead of coffee – it is thought that this beverage soothes and fortifies the nervous system as well as being very refreshing.

Barley is found either hulled or pearled in the market. Hulled or whole-grain barley has only the outer covering removed, leaving the inner covering of the seed, it is the most nutritious of the two types. Pearl barley has had the bran removed (the inner shell) and it has been steamed and polished. This process is also applied to rice, and considerably impoverishes the natural product: barley is a good source of B vitamins, potassium, phosphorus and magnesium, but most of the B vitamins and fibre are found in the bran.

If possible, serve barley in the liquid in which it is cooked because the B vitamins it contains are water-soluble. If you cook barley until it starts to break up, for example in a soup, it will become very creamy and act as a thickener.

Buckwheat
GRANOSARACENO

Strictly speaking, buckwheat, with its triangular shape, is not a cereal grain. Yet it is always associated with the cereal family, which it resembles so closely in its nutritive benefits, being rich in iron, vitamins E and B, and magnesium. Reassuringly, buckwheat is never chemically forced to grow, as this makes the leaves too big at the expense of the seeds, so you can always be sure of its origins. In Valtellina, an Alpine

region in north Italy, one of the local specialities is a pasta made with a combination of buckwheat and wheat flour called *pizzoccheri*. Very hearty and delicious, it is served with cheese and cabbage.

The hulled crushed kernels, called kasha or buckwheat groats, are cooked very like rice. Wash well, then toast in a dry saucepan for a few minutes, till the characteristic nutty aroma is released. Add to twice its volume of boiling salted water and it will be ready in 20 minutes. Wherever millet is used in these recipes, buckwheat can be substituted.

Corn

MAIS

This cereal grain, also called maize, yields a delicious vegetable as well as a flour, oil, animal feed and even whiskey. In Italy corn is almost exclusively eaten in the form of a flour, which is called polenta. Inexpensive food of the mountain peasants, the dish made from the flour is inextricably linked with the fireplace – in the little huts a pot of polenta was kept bubbling all day long, hanging on a chain over the open fire. The perfume of the burning woodsmoke, adding itself to the flavour of the polenta as it was patiently stirred, was an integral part of the charm of this dish.

To make polenta, boil three times as much water as you have flour, add the polenta flour in a fine rain and salt to taste, then cook for at least 20 minutes, stirring constantly. Polenta can be made into many delicious dishes. For example, slice it, season with tomato sauce and Parmesan cheese and bake or grill (broil), then top with a fried egg. Traditionally, peasants would pour fresh milk over it and eat it warm or as a cold porridge. This is still good today, especially if the milk is really rich and creamy.

Millet

MIGLIO

Millet is the grain with the highest ratio of nutrients to calories, so it's a shame so much is cultivated just to feed animals and pet birds. A natural beauty product, it is justly famous for its effect on the skin, hair, nails and teeth due to its high calcium content. It is also highly recommended for pregnant women.

Millet is very digestible. Its bland, slightly sweet flavour lends itself to use in many kinds of recipes, particularly those based on vegetables. Rinse it well before cooking. Toasting it in a little olive oil before boiling enhances the flavour. Add to twice its volume of salted boiling water and simmer for 20 minutes. If all the water has not been absorbed, just leave for a few minutes. Millet makes a very good addition to vegetable soups; in this case omit the toasting stage.

Rice

RISO

This ancient grain has been cultivated for at least 7000 years. It is thought to have arrived in Europe with Alexander the Great; however, for a long period of time, throughout the Middle Ages, it was considered a very great luxury. It was at this time that rice entered the Italian diet, especially in the north, where it is now farmed extensively in the fertile Po plain. Here the short-grain rice varieties most suitable for risotto have evolved; Carnaroli and Vialone Nano are the most prized in present times.

Brown rice is the entire grain; only the inedible outer husk has been removed. As a result it has more vitamins and minerals than plain milled white rice. However, enriched white rice may have more nutrients than natural brown rice. Whichever type of rice you use, they are all a good source of B vitamins and carbohydrate.

To cook brown rice, rinse it well, then place in a saucepan with twice the quantity of cold water. Add a few drops of oil, a sprig of rosemary and salt to taste. Bring to the boil over high heat. After 10 minutes reduce the heat to very low, cover and cook for 40-50 minutes without stirring. When cooked, leave the rice to sit, covered, for a short while before serving, as this way any excess water will be absorbed.

Spelt
FARRO

Spelt is quite similar to soft-grain wheat. It was much used in the past, but this century it has largely been ignored. However, with the new awareness of vegetarianism and the interest in traditional ways of cooking, there is a new wave of interest in this ancient grain. It is the magnificent town of Lucca in Tuscany that boasts the greatest number of recipes for spelt, as well as being already famous for the exquisite quality of its

olive oil. These are both important ingredients in an old traditional peasant recipe that has become newly fashionable (see page 72).

To cook spelt, simply proceed as you would with any other cereal grain: soak overnight, rinse thoroughly, add to double its volume of water and simmer gently for about 1 hour after bringing it to a boil over lively heat.

Wheat
GRANO

The most versatile of all the grains, wheat has been the principal grain of the Mediterranean basin since time immemorial. In Italy it forms the base for pasta, bread, pizza and pastry. In its whole form – as kernels or wheat berries – it is full of vitamins, minerals and protein; however, the more refined it is, the more the vital forces that make it so wonderfully nutritious are reduced. If you want to cook whole wheat berries, soak them overnight and simmer them in three times their volume of salted water over moderate heat for just under an hour.

DRIED VEGETABLES

Dried beans, peas and lentils – called pulses or legumes – are loaded with nutrients. They are one of our best sources of protein and carbohydrate as well as being rich in fibre, minerals and vitamins. As such they are a perfect complement to cereals, forming a nutritionally complete meal.

To combat the problems of flatulence, rinse the beans thoroughly. Bring them to the boil and boil for 10 minutes or so, then leave to soak for 4-6 hours. Discard the water, cover the beans with fresh water, and cook as the recipe directs. (Lentils do not require soaking before cooking.)

A secret in cooking pulses of all kinds is to add salt only at the end of cooking, otherwise they will toughen. To enjoy them at their best, season them generously, with herbs and spices.

BEANS *Clockwise from top left:* Chick peas, lentils, broad beans, borlotti, cannellini

Beans
FAGIOLI

Dried beans are very popular in Italy. The ones traditionally used are borlotti and cannellini. In Tuscany cannellini beans are baked slowly in a wood-fired oven and dressed just with the best olive oil in the world and a little pepper. The result is totally unforgettable, not least for the respect it accords the ingredients. Borlotti beans are perfect for soups, purées and side dishes mixed with vegetables of every description, especially tomatoes. When cooking dried beans, add a sprig of sage or rosemary.

Chick peas
CECI

Grown since recorded history in the Mediterranean basin, chick peas were a favourite of the Romans, who used to sell fried chick peas in the street. This dried bean is round and plump in shape, and the flavour is mild and nut-like. Chick peas are generously supplied with fibre, iron, potassium and B vitamins. They keep very well. Add a few sage leaves when cooking.

Lentils
LENTICCHIE

Lentils are traditionally served on New Year's Eve in Italy, to bring prosperity, and everyone eats at least a little bit. There are many kinds of lentils, from tiny to large, in a variety of colours. Their major benefit is their impressive quantities of protein: although not the same proteins as those in meat, they can be measured against the protein levels of steak when completed with a cereal dish. Depending on their size lentils can take anything from 20 minutes to an hour to cook.

FLAVOURINGS

Aromatic herbs and spices are precious little microdispensers of health and pleasure. They contain very concentrated essences that serve to keep us healthy by stimulating two of our most valuable senses, those of smell and taste.

In traditional Italian cookery there is widespread use of herbs, probably because they grow in profusion in meadows, gardens, and on coasts and mountains everywhere. Experimentation over the centuries has built up a wealth of flavouring partnerships that is enjoyed to this day at Italian tables up and down the country. It has also produced a canon of herbal knowledge, such as that cooking aromatic herbs with cereal grains makes them easier to digest. It has also given us herbal teas, or tisanes, with their many therapeutic properties.

In ancient times before the advent of artificial refrigeration, spices were used to preserve meat, because it was found that their antiseptic powers kept harmful bacteria at bay. Today we need not use spices in this way, but their traditional flavouring uses still survive.

HERBS *Clockwise from left:* Basil, thyme, oregano, rosemary, marjoram, tarragon, bay leaves

Bay Leaves
ALLORO

The bay is a tree that grows wild all around the Mediterranean. It was known to both the ancient Romans and Greeks. It is very easy to cultivate and its strong aroma, both spicy and mildly bitter, can find many good uses in the kitchen. A few bay leaves dropped into oil or vinegar to infuse will yield very interesting results. If you cut a slit in a potato, slip in a bay leaf, drizzle on a little olive oil, close and bake, the potato will take on a delicious flavour.

Bay helps to stimulate digestion and it has preservative and antiseptic qualities. In the form of tea, bay will help calm a cough.

Basil
BASILICO

In Italy there's always a pot of basil near the kitchen. In spring the baby plants, complete with roots, are sold in every market and everybody transplants them into pots for window-sill or veranda. The words 'basil' and 'tomato' are practically inseparable: they form the basis of so much Italian cooking, above all in the south. But, of course, basil is used on its own too – to season minestrone, make Pesto Sauce (see page 154), as a substitute for parsley in Green Sauce (see page 155), and to flavour cheese.

Basil is a delicate herb. Add it to a cooked dish just before serving, so it barely wilts. Shred it coarsely with your fingers – if cut it can blacken and become bitter.

Among its many reputed benefits are the powers to banish depression, relieve tiredness and stimulate the brain. The leaves also discourage mosquitoes and flies, which is another good reason to have a pot in your kitchen window.

Cinnamon
CANNELLA

Cinnamon is not widely used in Italy, as it is considered exotic, although in the Alpine regions in the north it spices apple and pear jams that are used in cakes and pies. Cinnamon sticks can be stored in a jar of sugar; they will give the sugar a delicious perfume, making it exquisite as a sweetening for teas, warm milk, yogurt and coffee.

Cinnamon is a powerful stimulant and antiseptic: a tea made with it will help fight off an attack of influenza. It is also reputed to have the effect of helping in childbirth.

Fennel
FINOCCHIO

This elegant plant, with yellow umbrella-shaped flowers from which we obtain fennel seeds, is commonly found in the dry and sunny countryside of central southern Italy. In Tuscany its characteristic flavour is much appreciated and finds a place in many favourite dishes, particularly those made with pork. In fact a local sausage even bears the name 'Finocchiona'. It is possible that the combination of fennel with fatty rich meat is not altogether happenstance, as this herb helps us digest the heaviest of foods.

Traditionally fennel tea has always been drunk by nursing mothers. Chewing a few fennel seeds before meals will calm the appetite. To make tea, simply boil a teaspoon of seeds in a cupful of water for a minute or two. Drink warm or cool. It is very thirst-quenching and refreshing.

Juniper
GINEPRO

The juniper bush is a familiar sight in the Mediterranean scrubland, where it grows wild in abundance. The berries are protected by short bristly thorns and are usually green in colour. It is only in late summer that they mature and turn their characteristic violet. Since ancient times these berries have been much appreciated for their numerous powers: principally those of purifying the blood and stimulating circulation. The essential oil is prized for massage, as it aids the body in eliminating excess liquid from the tissues.

Juniper berries have a very intense aroma and taste, pungent yet with a little note of sweetness. Its highly perfumed wood is one of those used for the traditional maturing of balsamic vinegar, which passes from wood to wood to attain its unique bouquet. In the kitchen the berries are used to spice cabbage and beetroots for pickling.

Marjoram
MAGGIORANA

One of the oregano family, marjoram is very similar in taste to oregano, though a little sweeter and less intense. It is a small bush with pretty little leaves that grows in hot countries. Its flavour lies somewhere between thyme and oregano, so can be substituted for either one. It is wonderful in stuffings, in minestrone and with many vegetables, especially tomatoes and aubergines (eggplants). Like many other aromatic plants, it has been mythologized throughout history. Therapeutically it has a calming effect on the nervous system; the essential oil protects against anxiety and helps to ease muscle pain when used in massage.

Mint

MENTA

There are more than twenty different varieties of this powerful aromatic. One of the best-known is peppermint, which has a very pleasant freshness. Mint is commonly used to flavour omelettes and other egg dishes, adding its distinctive and stimulating taste. Mixed with plain yogurt and a clove of garlic it makes an excellent dressing for cucumbers, potatoes, tomatoes and courgettes (zucchini). Left to infuse in vinegar for even a short time it adds a piquant edge, making the vinegar ideal for marinating meat or fish.

Drunk as a tea mint has a calming effect on coughs and inflammations of the mouth. To make mint tea, boil a bunch of leaves in hot water for a few minutes, remove them, sweeten the tea with a little honey and serve hot or iced. A sprig of mint placed in a glass pitcher of iced water makes a perfumed and refreshing addition.

Nutmeg

NOCE MOSCATA

This spice is native to the Moluccan Islands, and was imported into Europe by the Arabs. In Italy its use was assured as the magic seasoning for béchamel, the finishing touch that makes that sauce what it is. Béchamel is used most often with vegetables 'au gratin' and in baked pasta dishes. For the latter, the béchamel is often liberally mixed with tomato sauce, covered with grated Parmesan and fontina cheese and baked to form a crust. Nutmeg-perfumed béchamel also makes a wonderful topping for mashed potatoes.

This spice gives an interesting dimension to minestrone, and goes spectacularly well in a risotto. Among garden vegetables, it combines well with pumpkin, turnips and carrots – all slightly sweet in taste. Fruits benefit from nutmeg too, namely apples, pears and plums, especially if baked in the oven with a little butter or cream.

Oregano

ORIGANO

This very aromatic little herb is common on the dry slopes of the Mediterranean mountainsides. Even dried it evokes images of warmth, sunshine and the sea.

In the kitchen oregano is very popular. The most basic, classic pizza of all is simply topped with tomato and oregano. A pinch of oregano adds life to any sauce or vegetable dish. It has digestive properties as well. Modern research has also shown that the essential oil is antiseptic and antibacterial.

Poppy

PAPAVERO

This marvellous flower, with its intense hues, has few equals in its power to delight the eye. One of the most sensitive wildflowers, the poppy suffers immediately from ecological imbalance, so there is all the more reason to be joyful on seeing its flowers, knowing them to be a sign of environmental respect.

In the Alpine regions of northern Italy poppy seeds are used to stuff an exquisite type of tortelli. Sprouted poppy seeds are delicious in soups, risottos and omelettes.

An infusion of poppy can be used for its notable sleep-inducing properties. For tea, you need only add a few petals to a cup of hot water. Sweeten with acacia honey.

Rosemary
ROSMARINO

Rosemary is one of the most common herbs of the Mediterranean basin. Its very intense aroma is enjoyed in a huge number of dishes, especially in Tuscany where it is used in breads, flatbreads and even sweets (see Castagnaccio on page 140).

Rosemary essential oil is an astringent. A few drops in the bath will help you feel refreshed after exercise. Like all the aromatics, rosemary essence is highly energizing so it is wiser to use it in the morning.

Saffron
ZAFFERANO

Saffron has been known in Italy since ancient times. Legend has it that while Milan cathedral was being built during the Middle Ages, saffron was used as colouring for some of the decorations; one day a little saffron dust fell from the ceiling into one of the workmen's plate of rice – and thus was born the famous Risotto alla Milanese!

The yellow colouring it imparts has always fascinated chefs, and saffron has found its way into many soups and minestrone. One way to use it is to dissolve a pinch in some water and add it to the water for cooking pasta. The pasta will emerge a decorative yellow colour, particularly suitable for cold pasta salads.

Sage
SALVIA

The name of this herb comes from the Latin word meaning salvation, for even the Romans were aware of its numerous healing properties. Sage has a strong and penetrating aroma, and its taste is a little on the bitter side. It is this bitterness that stimulates digestion and purifies the blood and its filters, such as the liver and pancreas. If you have eaten too rich a meal, a cup of warm sage tea can be a great relief.

Sage is much appreciated in Italian cooking. With a little garlic and ricotta it makes a great stuffing for pasta. It is also used often with meat and fish.

Tarragon
DRAGONCELLO

Tarragon, though not indigenous to Italy, is cultivated in some parts of the country. It is an extremely interesting herb, excellent in marinades. Left to infuse in good-quality white wine vinegar it adds a pleasant aroma, making the vinegar perfect for dressing green salads and boiled potatoes. Tarragon also marries well with eggs and in mayonnaise it is truly exceptional.

Thyme
TIMO

A graceful little evergreen bush that grows in dry and sunny places, especially in southern Italy, thyme has always been known for its stimulating properties. The herb is harvested before it flowers when the perfume in its leaves is most potent. A handful of thyme gives a special flavour to broths and soups and can make egg dishes both tastier and more digestible. An interesting addition to such pasta dishes as spaghetti, pizza or tortelli stuffing, thyme has a magical effect on tomatoes, as a mere pinch of the herb instantly conjures up the joys of summer.

SPICES *Left to right:* Cinnamon, nutmeg, juniper berries, saffron

PROTEIN

Although meat and fish have been included in the human diet for many thousands of years, it is perfectly possible to thrive without them. It is true that both contain many valuable nutrients, especially easily assimilable iron, but in the main we eat far larger amounts of animal protein than we actually need. However, if you are tempted to eliminate meat and fish altogether you should make sure you include other forms of protein in your diet, such as cheese, eggs, pulses, nuts and seeds.

Protein is made of amino acids, and different proteins contain different combinations of amino acids. Our bodies can make most of the amino acids we need, but there are nine, known as 'essential amino acids' that we have to obtain from the food we eat. Foods of animal origin – meat, eggs, dairy products – contain all the essential amino acids, which is why they provide 'complete' protein. Plant foods, on the other hand, yield 'incomplete' protein and so must be eaten in combination with each other to complete the necessary amino acid mix. This is simpler than it sounds: try combining grains, such as rice or millet, with pulses; pulses with nuts or seeds; or plant proteins such as potatoes or rice with milk, yogurt, cheese or eggs. And don't worry too much if you don't follow this pattern at every meal. So long as you are eating a balanced diet that includes a wide variety of foods your health will not suffer in the least.

CHEESES *Top to bottom:* Pecorino, Parmesan, mozzarella

Cheeses
FORMAGGIO

The range of Italian cheeses is vast. They are made from cow's, sheep's and goat's milk, and they are enjoyed in many forms, from soft and fresh to hard and aged. The downside to eating cheese is its high salt and fat content, very high in proportion to its weight. Taking this into consideration, the healthiest choice would be fresh soft cheeses, as they are much lower in both salt and saturated fat.

Eggs
UOVA

Eggs are a very versatile food, indispensable in Italian cooking. They are the basis for mayonnaise and creams, home-made egg pasta and many other preparations. If possible, buy eggs from free-range hens because the flavour will be superior. Also, the fresher the better: the eggs will be more solid and have a much more intense flavour. Eggs are much easier to digest if cooked without fat.

Yogurt
YOGURT

Yogurt is the healthiest way to enjoy dairy produce: the bacteria that causes the milk to ferment has a healing effect. Yogurt has also been found beneficial in lowering cholesterol levels and in treating heart disease. Many commercial fruit yogurts are highly sweetened – better to add honey and fruit to plain yogurt. Yogurt is precious in the kitchen as it can help to cut fat in dishes. For instance, you can mix mayonnaise with yogurt and flavour it with herbs to make a delicious sauce for vegetables and salads.

DRESSINGS

The quintessential dressing for raw or cooked vegetables is simply extra virgin olive oil combined with vinegar or lemon juice and salt. This is what you'll find every day on every table in Italy, and we never get tired of it. All other dressings are only for special occasions.

Italians are very sophisticated about dressing. They want it to enhance the taste of the greens without overwhelming it. We always use a classic dressing of extra virgin olive oil, red wine vinegar and salt, finding it never loses its interest. The dressing should be made freshly at each meal.

Extra Virgin Olive Oil
OLIO EXTRAVERGINE DI OLIVA

The olive is a strange fruit, inedible in its raw state. It must be cured in a brine or pressed to extract its oil to be enjoyed. To obtain olive oil, there are some strict rules that must be observed, ranging from the type and husbandry of the olive grove to the climate that the trees are exposed to. If the weather is very warm the resulting oil will be greasy and lacking in flavour; a cold winter will yield light oil with a fruity aroma. Olives must be gathered by hand, because if they are mechanically harvested they fall on the ground, are bruised and start to ferment. Obviously this labour-intensive approach adds significantly to the price of the resulting oil. Olives must be pressed as soon as possible after gathering, without being transported too far because the bumping bruises the olives and they start to become rancid, which in turn raises the acidity. Pressing must be mechanical, not chemical; filtration must be natural or by decantation. All these precautions raise the costs of production of an authentic and superior extra virgin olive oil, but the investment will be more than handsomely repaid, in its extraordinary goodness and complexity of flavour.

Extra virgin olive oils are premium oils that need no purification after pressing. They have to meet very high standards of aroma, colour and flavour. A good extra virgin olive oil has an acid content ranging from 0.2 to no more than 0.4 percent.

Everyone should learn to identify a good quality olive oil – with a little practice it is quite easy. Pour a little oil into a clean glass and observe the colour attentively. It should be yellow gold with green highlights. Next appreciate the bouquet: it should

have a fresh smell, with a clean, vegetable character like artichokes, and a hint of fruit, like a banana. Finally taste it as you would a fine wine.

Olive oil is thought to be linked to the low rate of heart disease in Mediterranean countries. This is because it contains mono-unsaturated fats, which can help reduce blood cholesterol levels. Olive oil is also beneficial in aiding digestion and normal bone growth.

Vinegar
ACETO

It's important to be aware of quality with vinegar – a harsh, cheap vinegar will ruin a salad that it dresses. Good vinegar should be made from top quality wine – red or white or sherry. The best method involves percolating it through wood chips that have been impregnated with the correct bacteria to effect fermentation. Dripping slowly through the chips, the vinegar also picks up subtle aromas from the wood. Ageing should take place in small bottles, to assure a rich complexity in the finished product.

Balsamic Vinegar
ACETO BALSAMICO

Balsamic vinegar is an extraordinary condiment, invented in the magical atmosphere created by the long and misty winter months in two great northern cities, Modena and Reggio Emilia. Authentic balsamic vinegar must bear a label stating that it is 'Traditional Balsamic', and it is bound by law to come from one of those two cities. The process involved in making it is very long and complicated. The result is almost priceless, and the very best is sold once a year at auction.

This vinegar is matured in a succession of little barrels, each one of a different wood, yielding different notes to the flavour. The process can take decades. The vinegar gradually reduces in volume and is transformed into a thick velvety substance with a flavour that is indescribably gentle yet complex: a few drops can take you to heaven.

In Modena and Reggio Emilia another (non-traditional) balsamic vinegar is now being made. It is a very interesting compromise. Matured for less time, and somewhat diluted, the result is a valid product that can be very useful in the kitchen, for dressing salads and vegetables and giving its mysterious flavour to sauces. Unfortunately there is also a range of inferior products that really have nothing to do with real balsamic vinegar. They are cheaply made by adding caramelized sugar to vinegar. The giveaway clue to their false nature is the acidic aftertaste they leave in the mouth.

DRINKS

Drinking fruits and vegetables in juice form is a very pleasant way to enjoy their best qualities. Wine is traditionally served at the table, and to my mind a glass of wine with a meal does one the world of good. Beer, too, can be a very nourishing beverage.

Juices
SUCCHI

The amount of juice obtained from fruits and vegetables will vary considerably, depending on the juiciness of the produce and the efficiency of your juicer, but on average the measurements in each recipe will give you one full glass. For all the recipes wash and chop all the ingredients, then put them into a juice-extractor.

Carrot and Celery Juice

This combination is custom-made for slimming diets: it abates hunger and is of great benefit to the complexion due to its high vitamin A content. Combine 2-3 carrots, carefully washed, 2-3 celery stalks, a few drops lemon juice and 1 bunch fresh flat-leaf Italian parsley.

Carrot and Orange Juice

Fresh and very thirst-quenching, this juice helps flush toxins from the body, at the same time as being delicious. Add a few ice cubes and a sprig of mint if you like. Combine 1 orange, 2 carrots, carefully washed and a few drops lemon juice.

Tomato, Cucumber and Beetroot Juice

The striking red colour gives you an idea of its regenerating powers, due mostly to the presence of the beetroot. It also has a regulating effect on the digestive system. If you'd like it a bit more spicy, add half a garlic clove and a few thyme leaves. Combine 1 tomato, 1 cucumber, peeled and 1 small beetroot (beet).

Lettuce, Apple and Celery Juice

The sedative power of lettuce was well known back in the time of the Greek empire; it was nicknamed 'the eunuchs' plant'. Apples contain many elements essential for good skin health, and celery is so full of nourishment it could practically be thought of as medicine. Combine 1 lettuce heart, ½ apple, 1 celery stalk and a few drops lemon juice.

Wine and Beer
VINO E BIRRA

In Italy wine is thought of as a food, so intimately is it associated with daily nourishment. The maxim should be to drink moderately, but drink well. Choosing wine with your meal should be instinctive and there are no rules, as this is a matter of personal taste. Good wine should be in harmony with the food served with it, and one should feel free to experiment with different combinations.

Beer is made by fermenting cereal grains. Beer made with traditional methods, not over-filtered or produced industrially, contains many vitamins.

THE *recipes*

The Italian culture springs from the loveliness of the countryside, united with a pleasure-loving nature, refined over centuries. It manifests itself in a love for flowers, gardens, botanical parks and, above all, in an affectionate and creative respect for the produce of orchard and kitchen-garden. The changing of the four seasons, influencing as it does the vegetables growing in our green gardens, has a profound effect on the choice of menus for the different times of year – Italian cooking is always in harmony with the ancient cycles of fallow and fertility in the earth, availing itself always of the freshest of produce.

There are marvellous culinary adventures to be experienced in fine restaurants, with master chefs in their kitchens. But the cook at home faces a greater challenge: that of creating every meal, day after day, and producing dishes that look and taste delicious without taking up too much time, that most precious of ingredients. To do this, all you need is a little organization – and a few tricks.

antipasti

As a rule we don't serve antipasti every day. Unless it's a birthday or some other special occasion, it is extremely rare in my family to find a meal beginning in this way. If we are receiving company, whether the group be large or small, we will serve an appetizer. In the old days meals were considerably longer, richer and more involved. I remember, in my child-hood, when eating at Coltibuono with my grandmother, there would be three courses plus a choice of a few vegetables as accompaniment. Sometimes these vegetables would take the place of antipasti. This happens often in summer, when one eats less due to the heat.

To simplify the serving of food at a sit-down supper, we tend to put the antipasti on the table before the guests are seated. On other occasions, the antipasti may be served with an aperitif; crostini are perfect for this. We serve them on a tray, with paper napkins, to accom-pany a glass of chilled white wine. In this way the early guests can have something to nibble on while waiting for the other guests to arrive.

For a really large reception or a stand-up buffet, there will be a grand assortment of both hot and cold antipasti, many to be eaten with the fingers. Mozzarella *bocconcini* will often make an appearance next to a wide array of tempting vegetables. The dishes will stimulate the guests' appetites and provide a very pleasing visual welcome.

What counts most with antipasti is the presentation. Garnish plays a large part in composing a successful appetizer course. Here you will find herbs to be valuable allies (I have a passion for fresh thyme and marjoram). If you can find little sprigs or leaves of fresh herbs, their aroma and appearance will add freshness and grace to your food. In summer a classic touch is to add a leaf of fresh basil or mint. Small olives, capers, slices of hard-boiled egg, lemon wedges and carrot or celery sticks can all be extremely useful too. In our garden there are many old grapevines that grow over supports to create shady bowers; I love to use the leaves to garnish dishes, especially in the autumn when the colours turn so richly beautiful.

Broccoli Bruschetta

BRUSCHETTA DI BROCCOLI

8 broccoli florets
4 slices coarse-textured whole
wheat bread, toasted
2 garlic cloves
4 tbsp extra virgin olive oil
Salt and pepper

Rustic and robust, this is a variation of the classic bruschetta made with
bread, garlic and oil.

Steam the broccoli for about 10 minutes or until tender. Cut each floret in half lengthwise and keep warm.

Rub the toast with the garlic cloves and moisten with a little oil. Arrange 4 pieces of broccoli on each slice. Season to taste, drizzle with the remaining oil and serve.
Serves 4.

Pepper Bruschetta

BRUSCHETTA DI PEPERONI

1 yellow sweet (bell) pepper
1 red sweet (bell) pepper
4 slices coarse-textured country
bread, toasted
1 garlic clove, halved
1 tbsp chopped fresh flat-leaf
Italian parsley
Salt and pepper
4 tbsp extra virgin olive oil

Baking sweet peppers in the oven really brings out the best in them. Apart
from serving them on toast, they are delicious by themselves, in
which case try rubbing their serving dish with a garlic clove. In this way the
garlic aroma will be moderate, rather than overpowering.

Preheat the oven to 180°C/350°F/Gas 4. Bake the peppers on a baking sheet for about 30 minutes, turning them over about halfway through cooking. Remove, wrap in cloth for a few minutes until cool enough to handle, then peel and remove the seeds. Slice into strips.

Rub the toast with the garlic clove. Arrange the pepper strips on top, sprinkle with the parsley and salt and pepper to taste, and drizzle with the oil. Serve immediately.
Serves 4.

Tomatoes with Mozzarella

POMODORI E MOZZARELLA

450g/1lb firm cherry tomatoes,
halved
350g/12oz mozzarella cheese,
cut into 1 cm/½ inch cubes
2 tbsp capers
8-10 black olives
2 tbsp dried oregano
Salt and pepper
4 tbsp extra virgin olive oil

Not only useful as a main dish, this appears often as an hors d'oeuvre. The
simplicity of the recipe dictates that the ingredients be of the very best quality.

Combine the tomatoes, mozzarella, capers and olives in a bowl. Sprinkle with the oregano, seasoning to taste and the oil. Stir well and serve at once. *Serves 4.*

Broccoli Bruschetta

Baked Onions with Balsamic Vinegar

CIPOLLE AL BALSAMICO

8 small onions
2 tbsp balsamic vinegar
2 tbsp extra virgin olive oil
Salt and pepper

This is a very appetizing first course for a sophisticated dinner. It also works well as part of a buffet meal. Ideally, use fairly small onions.

Leave the skin on the onions. Preheat the oven to 180°C/350°F/Gas 4. Bake the onions for 1 hour. Leave them to cool until they are easy to handle, then peel off the outer skins and slice in half along a vertical axis. Using a sharp knife scoop out the insides, leaving a shell of two layers. Chop the scooped-out insides of the onions into pieces about 2.5cm/1 inch square.

Combine the chopped onion, olive oil, balsamic vinegar, and salt and pepper to taste in a bowl. Mix well and use to stuff the onion shells. Serve warm or cool, but not too cold. Serves 4.

Aubergine (Eggplant) Mould

SFORMATINO DI MELANZANE

240g/8oz fresh plum tomatoes, peeled and chopped (or use canned)
10 fresh basil leaves
Pinch of sugar
Salt
Extra virgin olive oil for deep frying
1 oval-shaped Asian-type (Japanese) aubergine (eggplant), about 150g/5oz, cut crosswise into 8 slices
120g/4oz mozzarella cheese, diced
4 tsp dried oregano

Very rich and tasty, this dish can stand alone as a first course. It is a slightly more elaborate version of Parmigiana di Melanzane, a very popular dish that is made in the same way, but in a baking dish.

Put the tomatoes into a saucepan and bring to the boil. Add the basil, sugar and a pinch of salt. (A tiny bit will be enough as the mozzarella already contains plenty of salt.) Cook over moderate heat, stirring occasionally, until all excess liquid has evaporated and the sauce is very concentrated.

Meanwhile, heat oil in a pan for deep frying to 180°C/350°F. Add the aubergine (eggplant) slices, a few at a time, and fry until golden. Drain on paper towels.

Preheat the oven to 180°C/350°F/Gas 4. Brush the insides of 4 small moulds, each 5cm/2 inches wide, with a little oil. Lay 1 slice of aubergine (eggplant) on the bottom of each mould. Top with a generous spoonful of tomato sauce, add a quarter of the mozzarella cheese and sprinkle with a teaspoon of oregano. Top with another slice of aubergine (eggplant). Bake the moulds for 20 minutes. Turn out and serve at once. Serves 4.

Tomato Bombes with Mayonnaise

BOMBE DI POMODORI

FOR THE MAYONNAISE:

4 egg yolks
Salt and pepper
500ml/16fl oz/2 cups extra virgin olive oil
250ml/8fl oz/1 cup plain yogurt
2 tbsp Worcestershire sauce
Juice of 1 lemon

FOR THE TOMATO BOMBES:

8 medium tomatoes, well ripened
Coarse salt
2 tbsp chopped fresh chives
2 tbsp chopped fresh flat-leaf Italian parsley
2 tbsp chopped fresh thyme leaves

This is an ideal first course for an elegant dinner. It looks spectacular if you choose tomatoes of equal size and cover them completely with the mayonnaise, which must be very cold so it clings.

To prepare the mayonnaise: Place the egg yolks and a little salt and pepper in a food processor fitted with a metal blade or in a blender. Give a quick pulse to amalgamate the ingredients. Keeping the machine running, add the oil slowly in a thin stream till the mixture becomes nice and creamy. Incorporate the yogurt, Worcestershire sauce and lemon juice. Chill for at least 1 hour or until the mayonnaise becomes cold and set.

Put a small saucepan half full of water to boil over a high flame. When at a rolling boil, add 2 tomatoes and blanch them for half a minute. Drain and immediately peel them with a small knife. Meanwhile, blanch another 2 tomatoes, and continue in this fashion until all are done.

Slice a thin cap off each tomato, discard the caps, and scoop out the pulp and seeds with a spoon. Sprinkle some coarse salt in the hollows. Turn the tomato shells upside down on paper towels and leave to drain for half an hour.

Discard the coarse salt, then mix the herbs together and sprinkle some on the inside wall of each tomato shell. Place them upright on a serving dish and coat the sides of each one with mayonnaise. Put the remaining mayonnaise in a sauce-boat and keep chilled until serving.

Serves 4.

Melon Balls in Mayonnaise

PALLINE DI MELONE CON MAIONESE

1 egg yolk
1 tsp lemon juice
Salt and pepper
125ml/4fl oz/½ cup extra virgin olive oil
125ml/4fl oz/½ cup lightly salted whipping cream, whipped until thick
2 ripe round melons

Here's a delightful dish for a sunny day. Be sure to choose ripe melons and keep them chilled until use.

Put the egg yolk, lemon juice and a little seasoning in a food processor. Give a quick pulse, then, keeping the machine running, pour in the oil little by little in a thin stream. Transfer to a bowl, carefully fold in the whipped cream, 1 teaspoon at a time, so the mayonnaise doesn't collapse. Refrigerate.

Cut the melons in half horizontally and remove the seeds. Using a small melon baller, cut out the flesh in little balls and place in a bowl. Scrape out the rest of the flesh from the melon and discard, then fill each melon half with a quarter of the melon balls and dress with a quarter of the mayonnaise. Serve well chilled.

Serves 4.

Rice-stuffed Peppers

PEPERONI RIPIENI

4 bell peppers
12 tbsp arborio rice
salt & pepper
2 cloves garlic
6 tbsp extra virgin olive oil &
1 tbsp for oiling the baking dish
3 tbsp fresh rosemary
3 tbsp fresh flat leaf Italian
parsley
4 tbsp capers, chopped
120g/4oz mozzarella cheese,
diced

An ideal first course. Choose peppers that are as round as possible.

Cook the peppers in the oven at 375°F/190°C/ Gas 4 for about 20 minutes.

Cut off the tops, divide into two parts and scrape out the seeds. Cook the rice in a pan of salted boiling water for about 15 minutes. Drain. Chop the garlic and rosemary and cook in a frying pan in the oil over a low heat. Add the rice, stir for a couple of seconds and then add the parsley and capers. Stuff the peppers with this mixture and sprinkle each with some mozzarella. Arrange in an oiled baking dish and return to the oven for 5 minutes before serving.
Serves 4.

Cauliflower Surprise

CAVOLFIORE A SORPRESA

1 medium cauliflower
1 tbsp vinegar
2 hard-boiled eggs, thinly sliced

FOR THE MAYONNAISE:

1 egg yolk
Juice of ½ lemon
1 tbsp French (Dijon) mustard
Salt
175ml/6fl oz/¾ cup extra
virgin olive oil

This would make a good cold buffet dish with Tomato Bombes with Mayonnaise (page 57), Potato Grissini with Sesame (page 152) and some fresh slices of mozzarella. The surprise is the cauliflower, which is hidden by the eggs and mayonnaise. Serve with a very sharp knife for cutting the cauliflower.

Clean the cauliflower and make a cross-cut in the base of the stem. Put in a saucepan of cold water with the vinegar, making sure it is submerged. Bring to the boil and simmer for about 15 minutes, or until tender but still firm. Drain and leave to cool.

To prepare the mayonnaise, put the egg yolk, lemon juice, mustard and a pinch of salt in a food processor. Give a quick pulse, then, keeping the machine running, pour in the olive oil gradually in a thin stream. Chill for about 1 hour or until set.

To finish, spread the cauliflower with the mayonnaise and cover with the hard-boiled eggs. Serve at once or keep in the refrigerator until needed. *Serves 4.*

Rice-stuffed Peppers

Pepper and Fontina Rolls

INVOLTINI DI PEPERONE

*2 red or yellow sweet (bell)
peppers
210g/7oz fresh goat's cheese
2 tbsp capers, chopped
3 tbsp extra virgin olive oil
2 tbsp chopped fresh flat-leaf
Italian parsley, plus more to
garnish
Salt and pepper
8 thin slices Fontina cheese*

This is a particularly colourful and attractive dish, perfect for the warm season. The contrast between the sweetness of the peppers and the slight acidity of the cheese is very pleasant.

Preheat the oven to 180°C/350°F/Gas 4. Bake the peppers on a baking sheet for about 30 minutes or until tender, turning them over halfway through the cooking. Remove, wrap in a cloth for a few minutes and then peel. Open the peppers, remove seeds and membranes, and divide each one into 4 pieces lengthwise. Place on a working surface.

Mix together the goat's cheese, capers, oil, chopped parsley and seasoning in a small bowl.

On each piece of pepper lay a slice of Fontina, trimmed to fit. Spread a layer of the goat's cheese mixture on top and roll up neatly. Serve garnished with a small bunch of parsley and eat with potato grissini, or serve simply with cocktail sticks (toothpicks).
Serves 4.

Crostini with Chick Pea Purée

CROSTINI DI PANE E CECI

*300g/10oz/1½ cups dried chick
peas
Bunch of fresh sage leaves
Pinch of salt
2 garlic cloves
125ml/4fl oz/½ cup extra
virgin olive oil
4 slices coarse-textured whole
wheat bread
2 tbsp chopped fresh flat-leaf
Italian parsley
Few pinches of paprika*

This is a very rich and nourishing first course, perfect for the cold season. For a more elegant presentation, cut the slices of bread into thirds.

Soak the chick peas in cold water for at least 12 hours. Rinse and drain. Bring a saucepan of water to the boil, add the chick peas and sage and simmer for at least 1 hour or until they are tender. Drain and reserve 250ml/ 8fl oz/1 cup of the cooking liquid.

Discard the sage. Place the chick peas, salt, garlic, and half of the olive oil in a food processor. Blend to a purée.

Toast the bread slices and set them on a dish. Moisten each slice with some of the reserved cooking liquid. Cover each slice with a quarter of the chick pea purée. Sprinkle with the chopped parsley, paprika and a tablespoon of olive oil. Serve immediately.
Serves 4.

Celery and Walnuts in Saffron Aspic

ASPIC DI SEDANO E NOCI

4 tsp powdered vegetarian gelatine
500ml / 16fl oz / 2 cups vegetable stock
Pinch of saffron
1 tsp lemon juice
4 tbsp finely chopped fresh flat-leaf Italian parsley
Salt and pepper
350g / 12oz celery, shredded into very fine strips
120g / 4oz / 1 cup walnuts, finely chopped

Supremely elegant, this salad in its pretty yellow aspic is perfect for very special occasions. It can be set in individual moulds, if you like. For an alternative, try shredded carrots or fennel with grapes, other delicious combinations.

Soften the gelatine in a cupful of the stock. Place over very low heat, add the saffron and stir until the gelatine has dissolved. Transfer to a bowl and add the remaining stock, the lemon juice, parsley and seasoning to taste. Mix well.

Rinse a mould of 1 litre / 1¾ pint / 1 US quart capacity and coat the bottom with a little of the stock mixture. Chill for about half an hour or until set.

Add the celery and walnuts to the remaining stock mixture and pour into the mould. Chill for a few hours, or until set.

To turn out, run the tip of a knife blade around the inside rim and wrap a kitchen towel wrung out in hot water around the mould. Place an upturned plate over it and then turn it upside down. Give the bottom a few sharp raps to help dislodge it if necessary. Serve immediately. *Serves 4.*

Herb Cheese Roll

ROTOLO DI FORMAGGIO ALLE ERBE

90g / 3oz / ¾ cup freshly grated Parmesan cheese
90g / 3oz / 6 tbsp mascarpone cheese
90g / 3oz / ¾ cup grated Emmenthal cheese
90g / 3oz Gorgonzola cheese
1 tbsp finely chopped fresh chives
2 tbsp finely chopped fresh oregano
1 tbsp finely chopped fresh basil
1 tbsp finely chopped fresh rosemary

A savoury cheese mixture in an attractive shape is guaranteed to please your guests. For an elegant buffet, try rolling it into a long sausage about 2.5cm / 1 inch thick, cut little slices, and serve them on slices of fresh peeled cucumber. An extra garnish for the rolled cheese is a sprinkle of paprika, which also adds an intriguing flavour.

Blend the Parmesan, mascarpone, Emmenthal and Gorgonzola together in a food processor, stopping before the mixture becomes too smooth.

Chill for a couple of hours to firm.

Mix together the chopped chives, oregano, basil and rosemary.

Roll the cheese mixture into a long sausage, then coat it in the herbs. Keep in the refrigerator until ready to serve. *Serves 4.*

Cabbage with Balsamic Vinegar

CAVOLELLA IN SALSA DI BALSAMICO

2 garlic cloves, chopped
4 tbsp extra virgin olive oil
2 tbsp balsamic vinegar
5-6 juniper berries
900g/2lb white cabbage, very finely shredded
Salt and pepper

For this recipe the cabbage should be sliced extremely thin,
like angel-hair pasta.

Fry the garlic in the oil in a frying pan over moderate heat until it turns golden.
Add the balsamic vinegar, juniper berries, cabbage and seasoning to taste. Raise the heat and fry for about 1 minute, stirring. The cabbage should be just hot and tender but still crisp. Transfer to a serving dish and serve immediately. *Serves 4.*

Glazed Onions

CIPOLLE MARINATE

30g/1oz/2 tbsp butter
700g/1½lb baby pickling onions (pearl onions)
1 tbsp sugar
125ml/4fl oz/½ cup white wine
2 tbsp vinegar
Grated zest of ½ lemon
1 bay leaf
1 cinnamon stick
Salt and pepper

This has always been a classic starter because of its capacity to awaken
the taste buds. To facilitate the peeling of the onions, dip them briefly
in boiling salted water first.

Melt the butter in a large frying pan over high heat, add the onions and sugar and fry for a few minutes, stirring well. Add the wine, vinegar, lemon zest, bay leaf, cinnamon and seasoning to taste and stir well. Cover and continue cooking for about half an hour or until the onions are tender.

Discard the bay leaf and cinnamon. If there is excess liquid, transfer the onions to a heated serving dish and keep hot, then boil the liquid over high heat until reduced to a glaze. Pour it over the onions and serve immediately.
Serves 4.

Ricotta Cheese with Pistachio Nuts

RICOTTA AI PISTACCHI

450g/1lb ricotta cheese
90g/3oz/1½ cups pistachio nuts, chopped
2 tbsp extra virgin olive oil
Salt and pepper

Serve this surrounded with fresh celery sticks, for dipping.

Mix together the ricotta, nuts and oil in a bowl. Season to taste.

Store in the refrigerator until serving.
Serves 4.

Cabbage with Balsamic Vinegar

first courses

It may well be that the reason Italian cooking has become so popular all over the world is its first-course dishes. It is certainly true that a simple plate of pasta, even if served every day, remains a miracle in its ability to satisfy and please us.

Whenever it seems a chore to create something for lunch, a bowl of pasta never fails to solve the problem. All our family love pasta and our favourite way to serve it – especially popular with the children – is simply covered with tomato sauce. The great advantage of pasta is its great versatility, so repeating a dish too often need never be a problem.

Here at Badia a Coltibuono we receive many guests and friends who come because of our fine wines. Among them are some of the most famous restaurateurs in the world. We make a special effort to provide them with dishes they have never previously tasted, especially pasta.

We rarely serve pasta at the evening meal. Usually the first course then is a vegetable soup, thick and rustic, or an elegant consommé. Or occasionally a risotto will be served.

Risottos are almost as versatile as pasta. They can be made with a wide variety of sauces and vegetable combinations. Without disparaging the wonderful quality of Italian cuisine, superb up and down the whole length of the country, there are very few restaurants where I would order a risotto south of Bologna. My Milanese grandparents introduced me to my first unforgettable risottos when I was a small child, and it is very difficult to find any that compare with those in my memory.

Pizza is a favourite food for children, and it holds its charm well into adulthood. For this reason we serve it often when many of our large family unite to eat together. Due to the number of relatives, this doesn't happen too often, though when it does, pizza is always a natural choice as it adds a festive atmosphere to any gathering.

While pasta, pizza, gnocchi and vegetable soups are enjoyed all year round, it would be very unusual to find polenta eaten at any time of year other than winter, especially if it were cooked in one of the traditional ways, with cabbage and beans.

Green Pea Soup

PASSATO DI BUCCE DI PISELLI

*1kg / 2lb 2oz green peas,
unshelled
1 litre / 1¾ pints / 1 US quart
vegetable stock
30g / 1oz / 2 tbsp butter
½ white onion, sliced
2 tbsp chopped fresh flat-leaf
Italian parsley
6 tbsp extra virgin olive oil
4 thick slices coarse-textured
country bread, cut into 1cm /
½ inch cubes
Salt and pepper*

A very tasty soup, this was fashionable during those times when nothing edible was ever wasted. Instead of peas with their pods, you could use broad (fava) beans.

Shell the peas and put to one side. Wash the pods, cleaning them well, then leave them to soak in fresh water for a couple of hours. Drain and put into a saucepan with the vegetable stock. Simmer for about 20 minutes or until soft. Purée them in a blender and set aside.

Melt the butter in a saucepan over moderate heat, add the onion and parsley and cook, stirring frequently, for about 10 minutes or till the onion is translucent. Add the shelled peas and a little water.

Cover and cook for about 20 minutes, stirring and moistening with a few tablespoons of water every so often, until the peas are tender.

Meanwhile, heat the oil in a frying pan over a high flame, add the bread cubes and fry until browned, stirring often. Drain on paper towels. Set aside in a warm place.

Add the purée of pea pods to the prepared peas. Simmer together for a few minutes, then season to taste and serve, accompanied by the croûtons. *Serves 4.*

Cream of Cucumber Soup

CREMA DI CETRIOLI

*2 cucumbers, peeled and cut
into thick slices
2 medium potatoes, peeled and
cut into pieces
500ml / 16fl oz / 2 cups milk
500ml / 16fl oz / 2 cups water
1 glass / ½ cup dry white wine
1 tbsp chopped fresh flat-leaf
Italian parsley
Salt and pepper*

Light and versatile, this creamy soup is equally delicious hot or cold. The method also works well with other vegetables; for example, fennel, celery or Swiss chard. If serving the soup cold, try substituting mint for parsley.

Put the cucumbers and potatoes in a saucepan and cover with the milk and water. Simmer over low heat for at least 10 minutes, or until the potatoes are very tender. Using a blender, purée the mixture, then pour it back into the saucepan. Add the white wine, bring

back to the boil and immediately remove from the heat. Add the parsley and season to taste.

Serve piping hot. Or, if serving cold, leave to cool, then chill for at least an hour.
Serves 4.

Green Pea Soup

Crêpes in Vegetable Broth

BRODO CON CRESPELLE

2 carrots, chopped
1 head (bunch) celery, chopped
2 courgettes (zucchini),
chopped
1 tomato, chopped
2 potatoes, peeled and chopped
1 onion, chopped
2 litres / 3½ pints / 2 US quarts
water
Salt
250ml / 8fl oz / 1 cup milk
120g / 4oz / 1 cup plain flour (all-
purpose flour)
1 tbsp extra virgin olive oil
Bunch of fresh flat-leaf Italian
parsley, chopped
90g / 3oz / ¾ cup freshly grated
Parmesan cheese
3 eggs
30g / 1oz / 2 tbsp butter, melted

This is a delicate, almost Oriental dish that makes a nice introduction to a
dinner party.

Put the chopped carrots, celery, courgettes (zucchini), tomato, potatoes and onion in a saucepan with the water. Bring to the boil and simmer for at least an hour or until the broth has reduced to half the original amount. Strain the broth, add salt to taste and keep warm.

Heat the milk in a small saucepan over moderate heat until it is barely warm. Place in a blender with the flour, ½ tsp salt, the oil, half the parsley, 2 tbsp Parmesan and the eggs. Blend to make a smooth batter.

Brush the bottom of a frying pan with melted butter and place over moderate heat. When the pan is hot, pour in a spoonful of batter.

Tip and tilt the pan swiftly to make a very thin crêpe. As soon as one side is golden, flip it over and cook the other side for a few more minutes or until slightly brown. Turn on to a baking sheet and keep warm in the oven. Continue making the remaining crêpes in the same way.

When all the crêpes are done, roll up each one and cut it across into very thin slices. Bring the broth to the boil and pour into a warmed soup tureen. Add the crêpe slices and the rest of the chopped parsley. Serve at once, accompanied by the remaining grated Parmesan.

Serves 4.

Cream of Cauliflower and Millet Soup

PASSATO DI MIGLIO E CAVOLFIORE

4 tbsp extra virgin olive oil
1 medium cauliflower, cut in
pieces
120g / 4oz / ⅔ cup millet
1 litre / 1¾ pints / 1 US quart
boiling water
Salt
2 tbsp chopped fresh flat-leaf
Italian parsley

The sweetness of the millet combines well with the taste of the cauliflower,
resulting in a soup that's truly unusual.

Heat the oil in a saucepan over a lively flame. When hot, add the cauliflower pieces and sauté, stirring, until lightly coloured. Rinse the millet well, then add to the cauliflower and cook over high heat for a couple of minutes, stirring. Add the boiling water and salt to taste. Cover and cook over low heat for about half an hour.

Using a food processor, blend the soup until creamy. Pour into a warmed soup tureen, sprinkle with the parsley and serve hot.

Serves 4.

Rice and Parsley Soup

MINESTRA DI RISO E PREZZEMOLO

*2 boiling potatoes, cut in large
chunks
2 tbsp extra virgin olive oil
Salt and pepper
1 litre / 1¾ pints / 1 US quart
vegetable stock
210g / 7oz / 1¼ cups white rice
2 tbsp chopped fresh flat-leaf
Italian parsley
15g / ½oz / 1 tbsp butter*

This light soup is traditionally eaten at family gatherings. It goes particularly
well before a light main dish of pecorino cheese and
fresh young broad (fava) beans.

Put the potatoes, oil, and some salt and pepper in a saucepan with the vegetable stock. Simmer until the potatoes are tender, then remove them with a slotted spoon and transfer to a plate. Mash with a fork. Replace in the broth and bring back to the boil. Add the rice and cook over a low flame for about 15 minutes, until tender.

Remove from the heat. Add the parsley, butter and seasoning to taste. Transfer to a warmed soup tureen and serve.

Serves 4.

Pasta with Chick Pea Soup

PASTA E CECI

*240g / 8oz / 1 cup dried chick
peas, soaked overnight and
drained
1.25 litres / 2 pints / 5 cups
water
3 tbsp chopped fresh rosemary
6 garlic cloves, 4 of them
chopped
7 tbsp extra virgin olive oil
Salt and pepper
240g / 8oz egg tagliatelle*

This is truly a classic of rustic Tuscan cooking. It is filling enough to serve as
a one-course meal, especially with a bottle of good Chianti Classico wine.

Put the chick peas in a saucepan with the water, rosemary, whole garlic cloves and 3 tbsp oil. Bring to the boil, then cook for at least 1½ hours over very low heat. When the chick peas are tender, remove half of them with a slotted spoon and purée in a food processor or food mill. Return to the pan, add seasoning to taste and leave to cook over very low heat.

Meanwhile, cook the tagliatelle in plenty of boiling salted water, draining it when it is little more than half cooked. Add to the chick peas. Season to taste.

Heat the remaining oil in a little saucepan over a lively heat, add the chopped garlic and fry for a few minutes until crisp.

Transfer the chick pea and pasta soup to a warmed soup tureen, pour the garlic oil over the top and serve.

Serves 4.

Pumpkin and Bean Soup

ZUPPA DI FAGIOLI E ZUCCA

350g / 12oz / 2 cups dried
borlotti beans
900g / 2lb pieces from a
hollowed-out pumpkin
4-5 boiling potatoes, peeled and
cut into pieces
Salt and pepper
125ml / 4fl oz / ½ cup extra
virgin olive oil
1 red onion, sliced
3 garlic cloves, sliced
10 fresh sage leaves, chopped
1 celery stalk, sliced

One attractive way to serve this warming winter soup is in the hollowed pumpkin shell itself, heated in the oven. Serve more extra virgin olive oil as an accompaniment, so everyone can help themselves to as much as they like.

Soak the beans in cold water for 12 hours, changing the water a couple of times if possible. Rinse and drain. Put them in a saucepan and add water to come 2.5cm/1 inch above the level of the beans. Bring to a simmer over a low flame.

Add the pumpkin, potatoes and cook over low heat for 2-3 hours, until very tender. Mash the pumpkin and potatoes with a fork to thicken the soup. Turn off the heat and let the soup cook for 5-10 minutes longer with the remaining heat. Add salt and pepper to taste.

Meanwhile, place the oil in a saucepan over moderate heat. Fry the onion, garlic, sage and celery until they turn a little golden. Add to the soup and stir in well. Transfer to a warmed soup tureen and serve hot. *Serves 4.*

Lentil Soup

MINESTRA DI LENTICCHIE

4 tbsp extra virgin olive oil
1 onion, chopped
2 celery stalks, chopped
2 carrots, roughly chopped
Bunch of fresh sage leaves
1 bay leaf
210g / 7oz / 1 cup canned plum
tomatoes, drained and chopped
240g / 8oz / 1 cup lentils
1 litre / 1¾ pints / 1 US quart
water, plus 125ml / 4fl oz / ½ cup
water
Salt and pepper

This is a classic rustic Italian dish. Its success depends on the quality of the lentils, which should be of the large, floury variety.

Heat the oil in a saucepan over a medium flame. Add the onion and cook for a few minutes, stirring with a wooden spoon. Add the celery, carrots, sage and bay leaf. Raise the heat and cook for a few minutes, then add the tomatoes. Lower the heat and cook for a few minutes longer. Add the lentils and water. Cook gently for about an hour, partly covered.

Remove the sage and bay leaves. Add seasoning to taste and more water if necessary. Transfer to a warmed soup tureen and serve. *Serves 4.*

Pumpkin and Bean Soup

Cream of Cannellini Bean Soup with Sage and Lemon

PASSATO DI FAGIOLI, SALVIA E LIMONE

210g / 7oz / 1 cup dried cannellini or other white beans
1.25 litres / 2 pints / 5 cups water
20 fresh sage leaves
Salt and pepper
Juice of 1 lemon
125ml / 4fl oz / ½ cup extra virgin olive oil
4 garlic cloves, chopped

To avoid any risk at all of indigestion, use a potato ricer (food mill) rather than a food processor to purée the beans.

Soak the beans in cold water for 12 hours, changing the water 2 or 3 times if possible. Rinse and drain, then place the beans and measured water in a saucepan with a few of the sage leaves. Bring to the boil and simmer for about 1½ hours, until very tender. Add salt to taste, then purée with a potato ricer (food mill) or in a food processor. Add the lemon juice and place over very low heat. Meanwhile, put the oil in a frying pan over moderate heat. As soon as it is hot add the remaining sage leaves and the garlic. Fry for about 5 minutes or until crisp. Add to the soup and season to taste. Serve in a warmed soup tureen.
Serves 4.

Bean and Spelt Soup

ZUPPA DI FAGIOLI E FARRO

210g / 7oz / 1 cup dried borlotti beans, soaked overnight and drained
6 tbsp extra virgin olive oil
1 onion, chopped
125ml / 4fl oz / ½ cup canned plum tomatoes, drained and chopped
210g / 7oz spelt, soaked in water for a couple of hours to soften and drained
1 litre / 1¾ pints / 1 US quart water
Salt and pepper
1 garlic clove, very finely chopped

Spelt is a tender grain that is grown in the area of Lucca, in Tuscany. To cook it, follow the same procedure as for rice. The raw garlic in this recipe is for true garlic lovers.

Put the beans in a large saucepan, cover with water and simmer for a good hour or until they are tender. Drain, then blend until creamy in a food processor or a food mill.
Heat 4 tbsp oil in a large saucepan, add the onion and fry for a few minutes over high heat, stirring with a wooden spoon. Add the tomatoes and fry for a minute or two more, then add the spelt and water. Cook for about 40 minutes, adding more water if necessary. Season to taste.
Reheat the bean purée and stir into the soup. Pour into a warmed tureen. Dress with a thin stream of the remaining olive oil, sprinkle with the garlic and mix well. Serve immediately. *Serves 4.*

Onion and Mushroom Soup

MINESTRA DI CIPOLLE E FUNGHI

60g / 2oz / 4 tbsp butter
60g / 2oz / 6 tbsp plain flour (all-purpose flour)
1.25ml / 2 pints / 5 cups boiling water
2 white onions, finely sliced
6 tbsp plain yogurt
150g / 5oz fresh cultivated mushrooms, sliced
Salt and pepper
60g / 2oz / ½ cup grated Emmenthal cheese
4 slices homemade bread

This is a very tasty winter soup. If you'd like a more classic version, omit the yogurt.

Melt the butter in a saucepan over low heat. Add the flour, turn up the flame a little and stir with a wooden spoon for a few minutes, until the flour browns slightly. Slowly pour in 250ml / 8fl oz / 1 cup of the boiling water, stirring until you have a creamy texture. Add the onions, raise the heat a little more, and fry till they become golden.

Add the remaining boiling water. Stir in the yogurt and cook over a low flame for about half an hour. After about 25 minutes add the mushrooms, season to taste, and cook for 5 more minutes.

At the end of the 30 minutes, remove from the heat. Add the cheese and mix in well.

Place the bread slices in individual soup plates, ladle the soup over them and serve immediately. *Serves 4.*

Gemelli with Garlic and Mushrooms

GEMELLI AI FUNGHI E AGLIO

4 whole garlic bulbs
6 tbsp extra virgin olive oil
450g / 1lb fresh cultivated mushrooms, thinly sliced
2 tbsp chopped fresh flat-leaf Italian parsley
125 ml / 4 fl oz / ½ cup water
450g / 1lb gemelli
Salt and pepper

Instead of making the *soffritto* in the usual manner, the garlic is baked in the oven; the flavour is more delicate this way.

Preheat the oven to 180°C / 350°F / Gas 4. Wrap the whole garlic bulbs in foil and bake them for about 45 minutes. Remove and set aside to cool. Squeeze the pulp out of the skins and mix with half the oil. Set aside in a warm place.

Heat the remaining oil in a frying pan and fry the mushrooms for about 5 minutes. Add the parsley and water and continue cooking over a lively flame for another couple of minutes. Meanwhile, bring plenty of salted water to the boil in a large saucepan and cook the gemelli until *al dente*. Drain and place in a serving bowl with the garlic paste. Add the mushrooms, mix well, season to taste and serve. *Serves 4.*

Vegetable Minestrone Pesto

MINESTRONE ALLA PASTA E PESTO

*3 boiling potatoes, cut into
little cubes
100g / 3½oz / ⅔ cup shelled fresh
small green peas
½ cabbage, cut into thin strips
150g / 5oz green beans, sliced
3 courgettes (zucchini), cut into
little cubes
100g / 3½oz / ½ cup fresh
cannellini beans (if
unavailable, use dried beans
but soak overnight)
2 litres / 3½ pints / 2 US quarts
water
Salt
100g / 3½ oz / ¾ cup ditalini*

FOR THE PESTO SAUCE:

*60g / 2oz / ⅔ cup pine nuts
30 fresh basil leaves
2 garlic cloves
2 tbsp freshly grated pecorino
cheese
2 tbsp freshly grated Parmesan
cheese
6 tbsp extra virgin olive oil*

Any type of medium sized pasta will do for this recipe – for example, ditalini, maccheroni or conchigliette. For those of you who have the time, pesto can be hand-made in the traditional manner (the recipe can be found in the section dealing with sauces on page 154).

Combine the potatoes, peas, cabbage, green beans, courgettes (zucchini) and cannellini beans in a large saucepan. Add the water and a large pinch of salt. Cover and simmer over a very low flame for 2 hours.

To make the pesto, place the pine nuts, basil, garlic, pecorino, Parmesan and oil in a food processor and blend until creamy.

Bring plenty of salted water to the boil in a large saucepan and cook the ditalini until only half-done. Drain and add to the minestrone to finish cooking. Remove from the heat and stir in the pesto sauce.

Transfer to a warmed soup tureen and serve at once.

Serves 4.

Taglierini in Courgette (Zucchini) Sauce

TAGLIERINI IN SALSA DI ZUCCHINE

210g/7oz/1½ cups plain flour
(all-purpose flour)
2 size-2 (US extra-large) eggs
4 medium courgettes (zucchini)
125ml/4 fl oz/½ cup extra
virgin olive oil
3 sprigs fresh tarragon
60g/2oz/½ cup freshly grated
Parmesan cheese

This dish has a very delicate flavour. Tarragon is the ideal herb to use, although oregano can be substituted.

Place the flour in a large bowl with the eggs and beat lightly with a fork. Then, using your hands, work the flour into the eggs until a smooth, elastic dough is formed.

Using a pasta machine roll out the pasta dough to 2mm/scant ⅛ inch thickness. Cut into 5mm/scant ¼ inch wide strips.

Place the courgettes (zucchini) in a food processor and blend them, pulsing 4 or 5 times only, so they don't become too mushy. Turn the courgettes (zucchini) into a large saucepan and add 6 tablespoons of the oil. Cook over very high heat for 2 minutes. Remove from the heat and set aside.

Put the tarragon sprigs in a small bowl and pour over the remaining oil. Set the bowl over a pan of gently simmering water. Heat for a few minutes so the flavour of the tarragon is transferred to the oil.

Bring a large pot of salted water to the boil. Add the taglierini and cook until they rise to float on the surface. Drain and transfer to the saucepan with the courgettes (zucchini). Strain the tarragon-scented oil into the pan, add the Parmesan cheese and cook over high heat for just under a minute, stirring and tossing constantly. Transfer to a serving dish and serve. *Serves 4.*

Fusilli with Broccoli Pesto

FUSILLI AL PESTO DI BROCCOLI

600g/1¼lb broccoli
125 ml/4 fl oz/½ cup extra
virgin olive oil
1 white onion, chopped
1 garlic clove, sliced
450g/1lb fusilli
60g/2oz/⅓ cup capers, well
drained
12 fresh basil leaves
Pinch of chili powder
Salt

The word *pesto* refers to the way in which these sauces used to be made, back in the days of the pestle and mortar.

Cut off the broccoli florets and set aside. Peel the stalks and cut them into pieces. Bring a large pot of salted water to the boil. Add the broccoli stalks and cook for a minute. Drain in a colander, saving the cooking water and returning it to the pot.

Heat half the oil in a frying pan over high heat, add the onion and garlic and cook for about 2 minutes or until translucent. Add the broccoli florets and stalks, cover the pan and continue cooking over low heat for 20 minutes, stirring from time to time and adding a

few tablespoons of the reserved cooking water to moisten.

Bring the pot of broccoli cooking water back to the boil. Add the fusilli and cook till *al dente*. Meanwhile, transfer the broccoli mixture to a food processor and add the remaining oil, the capers, basil, chili powder and salt to taste. Give a few quick pulses.

Drain the pasta and turn into a serving dish. Pour the broccoli pesto sauce over the top and mix well. Serve at once.
Serves 4.

Multicolour Conchiglie Salad

CONCHIGLIE IN INSALATA

450g / 1lb conchiglie
6 tbsp extra virgin olive oil
8 cherry tomatoes, quartered
1 sweet (bell) pepper, diced
1 celery stalk, white and tender,
cut into thin slices
8 pitted black olives, sliced
30g / 1oz rocket (arugula),
shredded
8 fresh mint leaves, shredded
240g / 8oz mozzarella cheese, cut
into 1cm / ½ inch cubes
Juice of ½ lemon
Salt and pepper

This is a cold pasta dish, perfect for summer, when all the ingredients are at their peak of flavour. After cooking and draining the pasta, mix in a little extra virgin olive oil before leaving it to cool at room temperature in a large bowl. It is a mistake to cool it by running cold water over it, as this will cause loss of flavour and texture.

Put a large saucepan of salted water to boil. Add the conchiglie and cook till *al dente*, then drain. Place in a bowl, toss with half the oil and allow to cool. When the pasta is at room temperature, add the tomatoes, yellow pepper, celery, olives, rocket (arugula), mint and mozzarella. Mix well. Blend the remaining oil with the lemon juice, and salt and pepper to taste, using a fork, and pour over the pasta. Mix well.

If you prefer this dish chilled, let it sit for half an hour in the refrigerator before serving. *Serves 4.*

Angel Hair Spaghetti with Tomatoes

CAPELLI D'ANGELO AI POMODORI CRUDI

4 ripe tomatoes
450g / 1lb angel hair spaghetti
4 tbsp extra virgin olive oil
2 garlic cloves, chopped
1 tbsp chopped fresh mint
1 tbsp dried oregano
Salt and pepper

When making this recipe, take great care not to splash the hot oil on to yourself because at the correct heat it might spatter quite a bit.

Bring a saucepan of salted water to the boil. Drop in the tomatoes for half a minute. Drain and peel them while still warm. Cut them in half, remove the seeds and cut into pieces. Place in a strainer to drain off excess water.
Put the angel hair pasta to cook in boiling salted water.
Meanwhile, heat the oil in a frying pan and fry the garlic for a couple of minutes, till crispy and golden.
Drain the pasta while still *al dente* and turn into a serving dish. Sprinkle with the tomatoes, mint, oregano and seasoning to taste. Pour the hot garlic oil over the top, stir well and serve immediately.
Serves 4.

Multicolour Conchiglie Salad

Penne with Artichokes, Broad Beans (Fava Beans) and Peas

PENNE AI CARCIOFI, FAVE E PISELLI

3 young globe artichokes
1 tsp lemon juice
6 tbsp extra virgin olive oil
1 small onion, sliced
2 garlic cloves, chopped
120g/4oz/¾ cup shelled fresh broad beans (fava beans)
120g/4oz/¾ cup shelled fresh green peas
1 tbsp fresh thyme leaves
Salt and pepper
450g/1lb penne

If you would like, serve the vegetables alongside the pasta, instead of mixed into it.

Clean the artichokes and cut into pieces, removing the hairy choke. Place in a bowl with the lemon juice and cover with water to prevent discoloration.

Heat the oil in a large frying pan over moderate heat. Add the onion and garlic and fry for 7-8 minutes or until translucent. Drain the artichokes, pat dry with paper towels, then add to the frying pan and cook for 10 minutes. Add the broad beans (fava beans) and cook for about 10 minutes, then add the peas and thyme. Cover and cook gently for another 10 minutes, adding a little water and stirring from time to time. Season to taste.

Meanwhile bring a large pan of salted water to the boil and cook the penne until *al dente*. Drain and arrange in a heated serving dish. Add the vegetables, mix well and serve at once.

Serves 4.

Spaghetti with Garlic and Walnuts

SPAGHETTI AGLIO E NOCI

125ml/4fl oz/½ cup extra virgin olive oil
3 garlic cloves, finely chopped
6 tbsp breadcrumbs
90g/3oz/¾ cup walnuts, chopped
450g/1lb spaghetti
Sprigs of fresh marjoram
Salt

This is a variant of the classic 'oil and garlic' sauce. Very tasty and nutritious, it is a favourite for all seasons.

Heat the oil in a large frying pan over moderate heat. Add half the garlic and fry for a few minutes, then add the breadcrumbs and walnuts. Stir with a wooden spoon until they brown and become crunchy. Remove from the heat.

Cook the pasta in plenty of boiling salted water. Drain very well while it is still *al dente* and transfer to the frying pan. Shred the marjoram leaves and add them together with the remaining garlic and salt to taste. Cook a further few minutes, stirring often. Transfer to a serving dish and serve at once.

Serves 4.

Tagliatelle with Courgettes (Zucchini), Peppers and Carrots

TAGLIATELLE CON ZUCCHINI, PEPERONI E CAROTE

6 tbsp extra virgin olive oil
1 garlic clove, chopped
½ onion, chopped
4 courgettes (zucchini), sliced into julienne strips
1 green sweet (bell) pepper, cut into julienne strips
2 carrots, cut into julienne strips
Pinch of dried hot chilli pepper flakes (dried red pepper flakes)
1 tbsp dried oregano
Salt
350g / 12oz egg tagliatelle

This is an egg pasta, so you can serve smaller quantities because it is more filling. This dish shouldn't be too spicy – use a light touch with the chilli pepper. It makes a nice first course for a summer lunch.

Heat half the oil in a frying pan, add the garlic and onion and fry for a few minutes over moderate heat. Add the courgettes (zucchini), green pepper, carrots, chilli flakes and oregano. Raise the heat and fry for about 10 minutes, stirring. Salt to taste.

Meanwhile, put the tagliatelle into a saucepan of boiling salted water. Drain when half cooked, reserving 5 tbsp of the cooking water.

Add the tagliatelle to the frying pan and cook over a lively heat for a few minutes, tossing and adding the reserved cooking water from time to time to keep them moist.

Transfer to a serving dish and serve.

Serves 4.

Polenta with Leeks

POLENTA E PORRI

1.5 litres / 2½ pints / 1½ US quarts water
Salt and pepper
240g / 8oz / 2 cups polenta or yellow cornmeal
30g / 1oz / 2 tbsp butter
8 leeks, white part only, cut into thin strips
1 tbsp caraway seeds
210g / 7oz Fontina cheese, cut into cubes

This is a meal in itself. Mouthwatering and extremely filling, it is just the ticket for a cold winter's lunch.

Put the water and a large pinch of salt in a saucepan and bring to the boil. Pour in the polenta or cornmeal in a fine stream, stirring. Cook for about 20 minutes or until the polenta is very soft.

Melt the butter in a large frying pan over moderate heat and add the leeks and caraway seeds. Cover and braise gently, stirring from time to time, until the leeks are soft. Add the Fontina cubes, stir a couple of times and remove from the heat. Keep warm.

Pour the polenta on to individual plates in the form of a nest and spoon the leeks and Fontina in the centre. Sprinkle with pepper to taste and serve immediately.

Serves 4.

Overleaf: Spaghetti with Garlic and Walnuts, Penne with Artichokes, Broad Beans (Fava Beans) and Peas

Spinach and Ricotta Gnocchi

GNOCCHI DI SPINACI E RICOTTA

450g / 1lb / 2 cups ricotta cheese
450g / 1lb / 2 cups spinach,
cooked, squeezed dry and
roughly chopped
60g / 2oz / ½ cup freshly grated
Parmesan cheese
2 egg yolks (US large)
120g / 4oz / ¾ cup plain flour
(all-purpose flour)
1 tsp grated nutmeg
Salt and pepper
90g / 3oz / 6 tbsp butter
90g / 3oz / ¾ cup freshly grated
Parmesan cheese

The Italian name for these gnocchi is *malfatti*, which means 'badly made'. This relates to their shape, which resembles a small egg flattened a little at both ends. The flavour of these gnocchi is so delicate and complete that you really don't need a fancy sauce over them – a little butter and grated Parmesan are sufficient. A light tomato sauce is also quite appropriate. If you like you can make the gnocchi with whole wheat flour.

Combine the ricotta, spinach, Parmesan, egg yolks, half the flour, the nutmeg, and a little salt and pepper in a bowl. Mix well. Dust your hands with flour. Taking one table-spoon of dough at a time, form the gnocchi in the palms of your hands, making them into small ovals, longer than they are wide. Dust them with the remaining flour.

Bring a large saucepan of salted water to the boil. Drop in the gnocchi a few at a time. When they return to the surface, remove them with a slotted spoon and arrange them in a warmed soup tureen.
Melt the butter in a little frying pan, pour over the gnocchi and serve at once, accompanied by the Parmesan. *Serves 4.*

Gnocchi in Cardoon Cream

GNOCCHI IN CREMA DI CARDI

500ml/16fl oz/2 cups water
120g/4oz/1 stick (½ cup)
butter
Pinch of grated nutmeg
Salt and pepper
240g/8oz/1⅔ cups plain flour
(all-purpose flour)
150g/5oz/1¼ cups grated
Emmenthal cheese
4 eggs

FOR THE CREAM SAUCE:

700g/1½lb cardoons, cut into
pieces and covered with water
and a little lemon juice to
prevent discoloration
30g/1oz/2 tbsp butter
250ml/8fl oz/1 cup double
(heavy) cream
60g/2oz/½ cup freshly grated
Parmesan cheese

Gnocchi are very popular, simple to make and extremely versatile. Their particular texture marries well with the simplest of sauces, such as melted butter and sage, or an everyday tomato sauce. More sophisticated versions include mushrooms and melted truffle butter.

Put the water, butter, nutmeg and a pinch of salt in a saucepan. Bring to the boil over high heat.

Remove from the heat and add the flour all in one go, stirring vigorously with a wooden spoon so no lumps form. Replace over moderate heat and continue stirring until the dough turns into a ball. Remove from the heat and leave to cool. Mix in the Emmenthal and the eggs, one by one, stirring until the dough is smooth.

Bring a saucepan of salted water to the boil. Fill a wide-nozzled piping bag (pastry bag) with the gnocchi dough and squeeze lengths of 2.5cm/1 inch straight into the boiling water, cutting them off as they come out of the nozzle. As soon as they rise to the surface, remove the gnocchi with a slotted spoon. Rinse them under cold running water for a few seconds, and then lay them out to dry on a kitchen towel.

For the sauce, drain the cardoons and pat dry then cook in plenty of boiling salted water for about an hour till fairly tender. Drain.

Melt the butter in a saucepan, add the cardoons and fry for about 15 minutes over moderate heat, stirring often. Purée in a food processor with the cream. Season to taste.

Preheat the oven to 180°C/350°F/Gas 4. Grease a baking dish with butter. Arrange the gnocchi in the dish, pour the sauce over the top and sprinkle with the Parmesan. Bake for about 20 minutes or until the sauce starts to bubble. *Serves 4.*

Pizza with Mushrooms and Ricotta

PIZZA CON FUNGHI E RICOTTA

30g / 1oz / 2 tbsp butter
2 garlic cloves, halved
300g / 10oz fresh wild
mushrooms, sliced
Salt and pepper
30cm / 12 inch pizza crust
(page 86)
8 cherry tomatoes, quartered
150g / 5oz ricotta cheese,
crumbled

For this pizza dough I suggest the hearty flavour of whole wheat flour. If you'd like a change from making one big pizza, make four little individual ones instead.

Preheat the oven to 220°C / 425°F / Gas 7. Melt the butter in a frying pan and fry the garlic for about 5 minutes or until browned. Remove and discard the garlic. Add the mushrooms to the butter and fry over moderate heat for about 10 minutes or until browned. Stir occasionally, and season to taste.

Arrange the mushrooms on the pizza crust. Add a layer of tomatoes and the crumbled ricotta. (If the ricotta is creamy, simply spread it on to the crust.) Bake for about 10 minutes. Lower the heat to 200°C / 400°F / Gas 6 and continue baking for 10 minutes or until the crust has browned. *Serves 4.*

Pizza with Radicchio, Peppers and Olives

PIZZA CON RADICCHIO, PEPERONI E OLIVE

2 yellow sweet (bell) peppers,
halved and seeded
4 tbsp extra virgin olive oil
2 heads radicchio, quartered
30cm / 12 inch pizza crust
(page 86)
180g / 6oz smoked mozzarella
cheese, cut into cubes
4 garlic cloves, very finely
chopped
12 pitted black olives

If you prefer, use plain flour (all-purpose flour) rather than whole wheat; this will give you a lighter crust. Half whole wheat and half white flour works too. Smoked mozzarella is an interesting ingredient with a strong flavour; however, you can omit it – cheese is never essential to a delicious pizza.

Preheat the grill (broiler). Preheat the oven to 220°C / 425°F / Gas 7. Brush the pepper halves with a little oil and place them on a baking sheet under the grill (broiler). Grill each side for a few minutes until lightly charred. Repeat with the radicchio. Cut both into thin strips.

Cover the pizza crust with radicchio. Place a layer of pepper strips on top and scatter on the mozzarella cubes, garlic and olives. Drizzle with the remaining olive oil. Bake for 10 minutes. Lower the heat to 200°C / 400°F / Gas 6 and bake for a further 10 minutes or until the crust has browned. *Serves 4.*

Pizza with Radicchio, Peppers and Olives

Pizza with Onions and Pine Nuts

PIZZA CON CIPOLLA E PINOLI

4 tbsp extra virgin olive oil
4 onions, thinly sliced
2 juniper berries, crushed
30cm / 12 inch pizza crust
(see below)
Salt
90g / 3oz / 1 cup pine nuts

This pizza is also great made with leeks or fennel in place of the onions. If you'd like a thicker crust, make the pizza 24cm / 10 inches in diameter.

Heat the oil in a frying pan, add the onions and juniper berries and fry over moderate heat for about 20 minutes, stirring occasionally. Remove from the heat and add salt to taste.
Preheat the oven to 220°C / 425°F / Gas 7.

Cover the pizza crust with the onion mixture and pine nuts. Bake for 10 minutes. Lower the heat to 200°C / 400°F / Gas 6 and continue baking for 10 minutes or until the crust has browned.
Serves 4.

Pizza with Potatoes, Onions and Capers

PIZZA INTEGRALE CON PATATE, CIPOLLE E CAPPERI

FOR THE PIZZA CRUST:

1 tbsp dry yeast
250ml / 8fl oz / 1 cup warm water
350g / 12oz / 3 cups whole wheat flour plus more for kneading
1 tsp salt
1 tbsp extra virgin olive oil

FOR THE TOPPING:

2 boiling potatoes, peeled and sliced paper thin
1 onion, sliced paper thin
30g / 1oz / 3 tbsp capers
2 tbsp dried oregano
Salt and white pepper
4 tbsp extra virgin olive oil

Whole wheat pizza has a more robust texture and the flavour is more complete than if white flour is used. If you'd like this recipe a bit richer, try a handful of crumbled Gorgonzola cheese in place of the capers and oregano.

To make the pizza crust; dissolve the yeast in the warm water and set aside for 10 minutes or till bubbles form on the surface. Make a mound of the flour in a large bowl and scoop out a little well in the centre. Put the yeast mixture and salt in the well. Using a fork, stir in a circular motion to incorporate the flour into the liquid, mixing until a dough forms. Sprinkle a working surface with flour. Put the dough in the centre and knead vigorously for about 10 minutes: form a ball, squash it flat with the palm of your hand, reform the ball and so on.
Grease a plate with oil, put the dough on it and cover loosely with a sheet of cling film (plastic wrap). Leave to rise in a warm place for 1-2 hours or until doubled in volume.

Resprinkle the working surface with flour. Turn out the dough on to it and flatten with your hands, turning it around and pulling out the edges. Shape a round about 30cm / 12 inches in diameter and about 6mm / ¼ inch thick, a little thicker at the edges. Transfer to a baking sheet or pizza pan and leave to rise for a further 20 minutes.
Preheat the oven to 220°C / 425°F / Gas 7.
Cover the pizza crust with the potato slices and sprinkle with the onion, capers and oregano. Season to taste. Drizzle a thin stream of oil over the pizza, distributing it evenly.
Bake for about 10 minutes. Lower the heat to 200°C / 400°F / Gas 6 and continue baking for 10 minutes or until the crust has browned.
Serves 4.

Risotto with Champagne

RISOTTO ALLO SPUMANTE

30g / 1oz / 2 tbsp butter
½ white onion, very thinly
    sliced
300g / 10oz / 1¼ cups risotto
    rice, such as Arborio
4 tbsp champagne plus 1 bottle
750ml / 1¼ pints / 3 cups
    vegetable stock
100ml / 3½fl oz / 7 tbsp single
    (light) cream
60g / 2oz / ½ cup freshly grated
    Parmesan cheese
Salt and pepper

This is a splendid dish for a feast. The champagne bottle explodes and yields
its precious liquid to enrich the risotto. Don't worry about splashing the
guests – champagne doesn't stain.
The less adventurous can make this recipe by reducing the amount of broth
and adding champagne instead, slightly warmed, during the cooking.
Naturally, this way one is deprived of the climax. Try it with
Italian champagne.

Melt the butter in a saucepan, add the onion and fry over a low flame until translucent. Add the rice, raise the heat to moderate and cook for a few minutes, stirring often. Add the 4 tbsp champagne and let it evaporate, stirring.
Bring the vegetable stock to the boil, then lower to a simmer. Pour enough stock over the rice to cover it. Continue cooking for 15 minutes, adding more stock as the top of the rice becomes exposed. Stir frequently. Remove from the heat, add the cream and Parmesan and season to taste. Cover and let

sit for a few minutes.
Meanwhile prepare the bottle of champagne. It should be cold but not iced. Remove the foil from the top but don't unwind the wire that holds down the cork.
Pour the risotto into a warmed serving bowl and carry it to the table. Place the bottle of champagne in the middle of the bowl, pop the cork and let the foam bubble down into the rice. When the champagne has stopped foaming, remove the bottle. Stir in the spilt champagne and serve.
Serves 4.

Baked Rice and Peas

RISO E PISELLI AL FORNO

210g / 7oz / 1 cup plus 2 tbsp
    long-grain rice
210g / 7oz / 1¼ cups shelled fresh
    green peas
60g / 2oz / 4 tbsp butter
60g / 2oz / ½ cup freshly grated
    Parmesan cheese
Salt and pepper
210g / 7oz / 1¾ cups grated
    Fontina cheese

This is delicious as it is, but is even more interesting made with brown rice.
It's a matter of personal taste. If using brown rice, add the peas when the rice
is half cooked, about 20 minutes before the end.

Preheat the oven to 180°C / 350°F / Gas 4. Put the rice and peas in a saucepan of boiling salted water and simmer for 15 minutes. Drain, transfer to a bowl and dress with the butter and Parmesan. Season. Stir well.

Grease a baking dish with butter. Fill with the rice mixture and sprinkle with the Fontina. Bake for 20 minutes or until there is a nice crust on top. Serve immediately.
Serves 4.

Carrot and Pumpkin Risotto

RISOTTO CON CAROTE E ZUCCA

*120g / 4oz / 1 stick (½ cup)
butter
1 small onion, chopped
210g / 7oz / 1½ cups fresh
pumpkin, peeled and cut into
2.5cm / 1 inch cubes
4 carrots, cut into 2.5cm / 1 inch
cubes
2.5 litres / 4 pints / 2½ US
quarts vegetable stock
400g / 14oz / 1¾ cups Arborio
rice
90g / 3oz / ¾ cup freshly grated
Parmesan cheese
Pinch of grated nutmeg
Salt and pepper*

The special characteristic of this risotto is the way the carrots and pumpkin
are partially mashed into irregular shapes.

Heat half the butter in a large, heavy-bottomed saucepan, add the onion and fry until translucent. Add the pumpkin and carrots and continue cooking for about half an hour or until tender. Using a fork, mash the carrots and pumpkin a little, leaving them in irregular pieces.

Bring the stock to the boil in a large saucepan, then turn down the flame and simmer.

Add the rice to the carrots and pumpkin and cook for a few minutes over high heat, stirring frequently. Lower the heat and pour enough stock over the rice to cover it. Continue cooking for 15 minutes, adding more stock as the top of the rice becomes exposed. Stir frequently. Remove from the heat and add the remaining butter, the Parmesan, nutmeg, and seasoning to taste. Cover and let sit for 5 minutes. Transfer to a warmed serving dish and serve.

Serves 4.

Tomatoes Stuffed with Rice

POMODORI RIPIENI DI RISO

*8 round ripe tomatoes
Coarse salt
210g / 7oz / 1 cup long-grain rice
1 tbsp chopped fresh basil
leaves
1 tbsp chopped fresh oregano
1 tbsp fresh thyme leaves
1 tbsp chopped fresh mint
leaves
2 garlic cloves, chopped
6 tbsp extra virgin olive oil
Salt and pepper*

This is a classic summer dish. For best results it is crucial to use sun-ripened tomatoes and freshly picked, highly aromatic herbs. Another tip is to baste the tomatoes frequently with their own juices while in the oven. They are delicious eaten either hot or at room temperature.

Slice 'caps' off the tomatoes, using a sharp knife; set these aside. Using a spoon, scoop out the seeds and pulp, transferring them to a large bowl. Be careful not to tear the skins. Sprinkle the insides of the tomato shells with a layer of coarse salt. Turn them upside down on paper towels to drain. Add the rice, basil, oregano, thyme, mint, garlic, 4 tbsp oil, and salt and pepper to taste to the tomato pulp. Stir well, then set aside for at least an hour so the flavours can mingle.

Preheat the oven to 180°C / 350°F / Gas 4.

Empty the tomato shells of the coarse salt. Using a slotted spoon, fill them a little more than halfway with the rice mixture. Replace the caps on the tomatoes and arrange them in a baking dish. Strain the juices left from the rice mixture, add the remaining oil and pour over the tomatoes.

Bake for at least an hour, basting the tomatoes frequently with the juices in the dish. Transfer to a serving dish. *Serves 4.*

Tomatoes Stuffed with Rice

main courses

In the environment we grew up in, it went without saying that the main course was always meat-based. Times are changing, however, and now it is becoming more and more accepted to serve vegetable dishes instead as the main course. The increased variety and abundance of vegetables is partly responsible, but there is also an accelerating shift away from heavy meat-eating, as we learn that cutting down on meat does indeed have positive effects on the health. It would be an exaggeration to suggest that meat is about to disappear from the traditional Italian diet, but it is usually now reserved for special occasions. More and more often grain- and vegetable-based dishes are eaten as the heart of a meal.

I've devoted this chapter to grain- and vegetable-based main dishes; however, you could just as easily combine two or even three vegetable or grain side dishes to make up a menu that is original and delicious, and that will give your family great pleasure. We plan seasonal menus in harmony with what is growing in our vegetable garden. In winter this is only cabbage and cauliflower, so we avail ourselves of the choice down in our little local village, Gaiole in

Chianti, which boasts two vegetable shops. It's interesting to note that these shops, which up until recently were dark little places with a very poor choice of produce, have been re-modelled as airy, light-filled spaces, with a much larger assortment of exotic fruit and vegetables, showing how the tastes of the local people have changed with the times.

The recipes in this section include moulds, pies and baked dishes. Even at their most elaborate, none of these recipes takes an inordinate amount of time to prepare, nor will they pose any insurmountable challenges to the inexperienced cook.

These days nobody has all day to spend in the kitchen, even if cooking is a passion. Cooking can be a relaxing pastime, and it gives you the great pleasure of sharing the results of your creativity in a direct, immediate and quintessentially satisfying way. But time doesn't always allow such enjoyment, so my style of cooking has evolved, with timing and nutrition being the priorities. I am sure there are many others who share this view.

Swiss Chard Pie

TORTA DI BIETOLE

180g / 6 oz / 1¼ cups plain flour
(all-purpose flour)
90g / 3oz / 6 tbsp butter, softened
and cut into little pieces
3 tbsp water
Salt

FOR THE FILLING:

1.5kg / 3¼ lb Swiss chard
2 tbsp extra virgin olive oil
1 garlic clove, finely chopped
1 fresh hot chilli pepper, sliced
60g / 2oz / ¼ cup ricotta cheese
60g / 2oz / ⅓ cup raisins, soaked
to soften
60g / 2oz / ⅔ cup pine nuts
1 egg (US large)
Salt

Spinach or fresh wild herbs can replace the Swiss chard in this pie.

Put the flour and butter in a bowl. Using your fingertips, work together until crumb-like. Add the water and a pinch of salt and mix to a smooth, soft ball of dough. Turn on to a working surface, sprinkle with a little flour, cover with a kitchen towel and leave to rest for half an hour.

Generously grease a 20cm / 8 inch loose-based (removable-bottom) flan tin or tart pan. Place the dough in the centre and spread out with your fingertips, covering the bottom and sides evenly. Set aside.

Preheat the oven to 180°C / 350°F / Gas 4.

For the filling: Remove the white stalks and ribs from the Swiss chard. Simmer in a little salted water for a few minutes. Drain, squeeze dry and chop into small pieces.

Heat the oil in a large frying pan over moderate heat, add the garlic and chilli pepper and fry for a few minutes. Add the Swiss chard and continue to cook over high heat for about 5 minutes to evaporate excess liquid. Remove from the heat.

Mix together the ricotta, raisins, pine nuts and egg in a bowl. Add the Swiss chard mixture, salt to taste and mix well.

Prick the pastry case (shell) and bake blind for about 15 minutes. Fill with the chard mixture and bake for a further half hour. Allow to cool for 10 minutes, then remove from the tin and serve still warm.

Serves 4.

Swiss Chard Rolls

INVOLTINI DI BIETOLE

12 Swiss chard leaves, stalks
removed
60g / 2oz / 1⅓ cups fresh
breadcrumbs
60g / 2oz / 1½ cups freshly grated
Parmesan cheese
12 blanched almonds, chopped
2 tbsp fresh thyme leaves
Salt and pepper
7 tbsp water

This also works well with lettuce leaves.

Preheat the oven to 180°C / 350°F / Gas 4.

Blanch the Swiss chard leaves in boiling salted water for 1 minute. Drain, cool under cold running water and drain again. Lay out 8 leaves to dry. Chop the rest and combine in a bowl with the breadcrumbs, grated cheese, chopped almonds and thyme. Season to taste. Mix well.

Place a tablespoon of the mixture on each whole leaf, tuck in the sides and roll up into a little parcel. Sprinkle the bottom of a baking dish with the water and arrange the rolls, seam side down, in the dish. Bake for 15 minutes. Transfer to a serving dish and serve.

Serves 4.

Swiss Chard Pie

Potato and Pumpkin Pudding

TORTINO DI PATATE E ZUCCA

1 garlic clove, sliced
4 tbsp extra virgin olive oil
600g / 1¼lb yellow pumpkin
flesh, cut into chunks
300g / 10oz potatoes
30g / 1oz / 2 tbsp butter
4 tbsp double (heavy) cream
Pinch of grated nutmeg
60g / 2oz / ½ cup grated
Emmenthal cheese
Salt and pepper
4 eggs, separated

This exquisitely rich savoury pudding makes an elegant main dish.

Put the garlic and oil in a frying pan over a lively heat and cook for a few minutes. Add the pumpkin and cook for about 20 minutes or until tender, stirring occasionally.

Meanwhile, cook the potatoes in boiling salted water for about 20 minutes or until tender. Drain and peel.

Preheat the oven to 200°C / 400°F / Gas 6.

Purée the pumpkin and potatoes in a food processor. Place in a saucepan, add the butter and cook for 7-8 minutes, stirring often, until excess liquid has evaporated. Remove from the heat. Add the cream, nutmeg, cheese and seasoning to taste. Add the egg yolks one at a time, stirring well to amalgamate thoroughly. Whisk the egg whites to stiff peaks and fold gently into the mixture.

Grease a loaf tin, 20cm / 8 inches long, with butter. Pour in the mixture and bake for half an hour until set. Turn out and serve at once. If you don't want to risk turning out the pudding, bake it in a shallower oval baking dish and serve straight from the dish.
Serves 4.

Onion, Egg and Potato Cake

TORTINO DI CIPOLLE, PATATE E UOVA

4 tbsp extra virgin olive oil
600g / 1¼lb boiling potatoes,
peeled and cut into matchsticks
2 white onions, sliced and
separated into rings
90g / 3oz / 9 tbsp plain flour (all-
purpose flour)
6 eggs
Salt and pepper
175ml / 6fl oz / ¾ cup milk

This is very similar to a flat omelette, and is delicious and easy to make. If you want to avoid turning it over at the end, just bake it in an attractive ovenproof dish in a moderate oven and serve as is.

Heat half the oil in a frying pan, add the potato sticks and cook for about 10 minutes over high heat until tender and golden, stirring once in a while. Remove from the heat and keep warm.

Heat the remaining oil in another frying pan, add the onion rings and fry until translucent. Remove from the heat.

Place the flour in a bowl and add in the eggs one at a time, beating very well. Season to taste. Add the milk a little at a time, stirring thoroughly.

Turn on the heat under the pan of potatoes. Add the onions and pour in the batter. Cook over low heat until the base has a good colour, then flip over the cake and cook the other side. Transfer to a heated serving dish and serve. *Serves 4.*

Brussels Sprouts and Chestnuts with Thyme

CAVOLINI E CASTAGNE AL TIMO

18-20 chestnuts, shelled
4 tbsp extra virgin olive oil
300g/10oz Brussels sprouts
210g/7oz baby onions (pearl onions)
210g/7oz baby carrots
1 tsp honey
8 tsp balsamic vinegar
2 sprigs fresh thyme
Salt and pepper

This tasty dish, served with brown rice and Beetroot Salad with Young Spinach (page 120), makes a meal as healthy as it is delicious.

Pierce a small slit in each chestnut skin. Cover with water in a saucepan and boil for 15 minutes. Drain and peel.

Heat the oil in a frying pan and add the Brussels sprouts, onions and carrots. Sauté for about 5 minutes. Mix the honey and vinegar and add to the vegetables. Continue cooking for a few more minutes, stirring often. Stir in the chestnuts and thyme, cover and cook for a further 15 minutes. Add a few tablespoons of water every once in a while to keep the mixture moist if necessary. Season to taste. Transfer to a heated serving dish and serve. *Serves 4.*

Radicchio, Chicory (Belgian Endive) and Courgette (Zucchini) Gratin

RADICCHIO, ZUCCHINE E INDIVIA AL GRATIN

2 heads radicchio, quartered lengthwise
2 heads chicory (Belgian endive), quartered lengthwise
4 courgettes (zucchini), halved
60g/2oz/½ cup grated Emmenthal cheese

FOR THE BÉCHAMEL:

500ml/16fl oz/2 cups milk
60g/2oz/4 tbsp butter
30g/1oz/3 tbsp plain flour (all-purpose flour)
Salt and pepper
Grated nutmeg

Vegetables 'au gratin' are a delicious and easy solution to winter menu problems. Try cauliflower, Brussels sprouts, turnips, celery or fennel. If you prefer you can make the béchamel using olive oil instead of butter, and vegetable stock instead of milk.

Preheat the oven to 180°C/350°F/Gas 4. Grease a baking dish with butter. Arrange the radicchio, chicory (endive) and courgettes (zucchini) in the dish and cover with a sheet of foil. Bake for 1 hour, turning the vegetables over a couple of times. Remove and transfer to a plate to cool.

Increase the oven temperature to 200°C/400°C/Gas 6.

For the béchamel, melt the butter in a small saucepan over a low flame, add the flour and stir well. Stirring, gradually add the milk. Bring to the boil and cook, stirring till the sauce thickens. Season to taste and add a sprinkling of nutmeg.

Clean the baking dish, grease with butter again and arrange the radicchio, chicory (endive) and courgettes (zucchini) in the dish. Cover with the béchamel. Sprinkle with the cheese. Bake for about 20 minutes. Serve hot. *Serves 4.*

Baked Leeks with Fennel and Potatoes

GRATIN DI PORRI

300g / 10oz boiling potatoes
2 onions, sliced and separated into rings
125ml / 4fl oz / ½ cup extra virgin olive oil
Salt and pepper
450g / 1lb leeks, cut into strips
2 fennel bulbs, finely chopped
3 tbsp breadcrumbs

This is also fantastic made with cardoons in place of the leeks and fennel.
Look for these in Italian markets

Cook the potatoes in boiling salted water for about 20 minutes or until tender. Drain, peel and cut into slices about 5mm / ¼ inch thick. Preheat the oven to 200°C / 400°F / Gas 6.

Cook the onions in a third of the oil for about 10 minutes or until tender, stirring often. Add salt to taste. Transfer to a plate.

Add half of the remaining oil to the frying pan and cook the leeks and fennel for 10 minutes, stirring and adding a tablespoon of water every so often if necessary.

Brush the inside of a baking dish with a little oil. Arrange a layer of leeks and fennel on the bottom and cover with a layer of potatoes, followed by one of onions. Season to taste. Continue layering the remaining vegetables. Sprinkle with the breadcrumbs, drizzle with the remaining oil and bake for 20 minutes. Serve hot.

Serves 4.

Turnips au Gratin

RAPE AL GRATIN

30g / 1oz / 2 tbsp butter
600g / 1¼lb onions, sliced
600g / 1¼lb potatoes, sliced
600g / 1¼lb turnips, sliced
120g / 4oz / 1 cup grated Emmenthal or Fontina cheese
4 tbsp milk
1 tbsp dried oregano
Salt and pepper

This dish is a breeze to prepare – just pop it in the oven and forget about it until it is time to serve. As well as being convenient, it is easy to find dishes to serve it with, to produce a rustic and appetizing meal. Try it with button mushrooms instead of turnips.

Preheat the oven to 180°C / 350°F / Gas 4. Generously grease a good sized baking dish with the butter. Make a layer of onions, then one of potatoes, then one of turnips. Repeat till you have used all of the vegetables.

Melt the cheese with the milk in a small saucepan over low heat, season to taste, then pour over the vegetables. Sprinkle with the oregano and season to taste. Bake for about 1½ hours. Serve hot. *Serves 4.*

Stuffed Aubergines (Eggplants)

MELANZANE RIPIENE

2 aubergines (eggplants),
weighing about 450g/1lb
altogether
125ml/4fl oz/½ cup extra
virgin olive oil
1 garlic clove, chopped
1 red onion, finely chopped
210g/7oz Brussels sprouts,
quartered
Salt and pepper
60g/2oz mozzarella cheese, cut
into little cubes
1 tbsp chopped fresh flat-leaf
Italian parsley

Stuffed vegetables are delicious and very typical of Mediterranean cooking.

Preheat the oven to 170°C/325°F/Gas 3.
Cut the aubergines (eggplants) in half lengthwise. Make little incisions with the point of a sharp knife in the cut surfaces and brush each half with a teaspoon of oil. Arrange on a baking sheet cut side up and bake for about 40 minutes until tender. Remove. Using a spoon, scoop out the pulp, leaving 5mm/¼ inch thick shells. Keep warm. Cut the pulp into little cubes.
Heat the remaining oil in a frying pan over a lively heat. When hot add the garlic and onion and cook for about 5 minutes, stirring often, till they soften and begin to melt. Add the aubergine (eggplant) pulp and Brussels sprouts. Cover and cook over low heat for about 20 minutes. Season to taste. Add a few tablespoons of water every so often so the mixture doesn't stick.
Remove from the heat. Add the mozzarella and parsley and mix well. Fill the aubergine (eggplant) shells and serve. *Serves 4.*

Aubergine (Eggplant) Caponata

CAPONATA

4 small round aubergines
(eggplants), cut into cubes
(unpeeled)
Coarse salt
125ml/4fl oz/½ cup extra
virgin olive oil
5-6 young celery stalks, cut into
thin strips
210g/7oz green olives
60g/2oz/⅓ cup raisins, soaked
to soften
60g/2oz/⅔ cup pine nuts
30g/1oz/3 tbsp capers
2 tbsp vinegar
Salt and pepper

This is a Sicilian dish that is as tasty as it is good for you. Served with simple brown rice it makes a complete meal. It's wonderful eaten cool in summertime, and the longer the flavours have to mingle, the more delicious it becomes.

Sprinkle the aubergines (eggplants) with coarse salt in a plastic colander and leave to drain for about an hour. Rinse off the salt and pat dry. Heat 6 tbsp oil in a large frying pan. Add the aubergines (eggplants) and stir-fry until tender. Drain and place to one side in a bowl. Wipe the frying pan with paper towels and add the remaining oil, the celery, olives, raisins, pine nuts and capers. Cook for a few minutes until the celery is tender. Stir often. Sprinkle on the vinegar, raise the heat and cook for a few more minutes till it has evaporated. Add to the aubergines, season to taste and stir well, then serve. *Serves 4.*

Overleaf: Stuffed Aubergines (Eggplants), Aubergine (Eggplant) Caponata

Onions Stuffed with Spinach

CIPOLLE RIPIENE AGLI SPINACI

8 white onions, peeled
60g / 2oz / 4 tbsp butter
600g / 1¼lb spinach, steamed,
squeezed dry and chopped
Salt and pepper
90g / 3oz / 1 cup pine nuts,
chopped
3 tbsp freshly grated Parmesan
cheese
Pinch of grated nutmeg
3 tbsp breadcrumbs

FOR THE BÉCHAMEL:

30g / 1oz / 2 tbsp butter
30g / 1oz / 2 tbsp plain flour
(all-purpose flour)
250ml / 8fl oz / 1 cup milk

This stuffing is also wonderful for sweet (bell) peppers. Bake them for
30-40 minutes first to soften them.

Cook the onions whole in plenty of boiling water for about 10 minutes. Drain. As soon as they are cool enough to handle, cut off the tops and scoop out the insides and discard so you are left with little shells, 2 layers thick. Preheat the oven to 180°C / 350°F / Gas 4.

Place 1 tsp of butter in a saucepan and melt over moderate heat. Add the spinach, season and sauté, stirring, till excess water steams off. Set aside.

For the béchamel, melt the butter in a small saucepan, add the flour and cook, stirring constantly, until lightly browned. Add the milk, a little at a time, stirring, then cook till the sauce thickens. Never stop stirring.

Add the béchamel to the spinach together with the pine nuts, Parmesan and nutmeg. Fill the onion shells with the mixture and arrange in a greased baking dish. Sprinkle with the breadcrumbs and dress (dot) with flakes of the remaining butter.

Bake for about 20 minutes. Transfer to a serving dish and serve.

Serves 4.

Spelt with Turnips and Celery

FARRO ALLE RAPE E SEDANO

600g / 1¼lb turnips, sliced
4-5 celery stalks, sliced
2 onions, sliced
2 bay leaves
1 tbsp fresh thyme leaves
450g / 1lb spelt, soaked in water
for a few hours until tender,
and drained
2 tbsp extra virgin olive oil
2 garlic cloves, crushed with a
garlic press
Salt

Tasty and good for you, this dish is a fine complement to the lentils
on page 132.

Preheat the oven to 180°C / 350°F / Gas 4. Grease the bottom of a baking dish with a little oil. Arrange the turnips, celery, onions, bay leaves and thyme in layers in the dish. Cover with the soaked spelt and add enough water to cover the grains. Cover the dish with foil. Bake for about 1½ hours.

Remove the spelt from the oven. Mix the oil and garlic in a small bowl. Add the garlic oil and salt to the spelt to taste and mix well. Discard the bay leaves. Replace in the oven, uncovered, and bake for a further 10 minutes. Serve very hot.

Serves 4.

Onions Stuffed with Spinach

Oatflakes (Oats) with Spinach

AVENA AGLI SPINACI

210g / 7oz / 2 cups oatflakes (old-fashioned oats), soaked overnight in 750ml / 1¼ pints / 3 cups water
Salt and pepper
4 tbsp extra virgin olive oil
3 small courgettes (zucchini), sliced
1 carrot, sliced
1 celery stalk, sliced
300g / 10oz spinach leaves, chopped
60g / 2oz / ½ cup freshly grated Parmesan cheese

To create a complete meal around this dish, I suggest preceding it with a light soup such as Cream of Cucumber Soup (page 66), and following with a salad of carrots and rocket (arugula) dressed with oil and lemon juice.

Transfer the oats and soaking water to a saucepan and bring to the boil over high heat. After about 10 minutes, lower the flame, add a little salt, cover and simmer for about 50 minutes or until all the water is absorbed. Set aside.

Heat half the oil in a frying pan, add the courgettes (zucchini), carrot and celery and fry over moderate heat, stirring occasionally. After about 10 minutes, add the spinach and seasoning to taste. Add a few tablespoons of water and cook until the vegetables are tender.

Transfer to a bowl, add the oats, Parmesan and remaining oil and stir well. Serve. *Serves 4.*

Barley with Nettles

ORZO E ORTICHE

210g / 7oz / 1 cup pearl barley, carefully washed and soaked overnight in 750ml / 1¼ pints / 3 cups water
4 tbsp extra virgin olive oil
2 onions, finely sliced
210g / 7oz young stinging nettle leaves, chopped
60g / 2oz / ½ cup grated Emmenthal cheese
Salt

Take care to choose young spring nettle leaves for this recipe. When harvesting, it is obviously advisable to wear gloves.

Cook the barley in its soaking water: bring to a boil and simmer over high heat for 10 minutes, then lower the heat and continue simmering for about 20 minutes.

Heat the oil in a frying pan over a lively flame. Add the onions and fry for a few minutes. Add the nettles and fry for about 5 minutes. Add the nettles to the barley, gently stirring. Simmer, covered, for about 20 minutes more or until cooked. If there is excess water, uncover the saucepan and simmer for a further few minutes until it has evaporated.

Remove from the heat, add the cheese and stir. Season with salt. Let sit for a minute, then transfer to a serving dish and let it sit for a further 10 minutes or so before serving. *Serves 4.*

Millet with Spinach

MIGLIO AGLI SPINACI

60g / 2oz / 4 tbsp butter
300g / 10oz / 1½ cups millet,
carefully washed
750ml / 1¼ pints / 3 cups boiling
water
2 white onions, thinly sliced
240g / 8oz spinach, finely
shredded
1 tbsp flour
250ml / 8fl oz / 1 cup warm milk
Salt
Pinch of grated nutmeg
2 tbsp freshly grated Parmesan
cheese

This also works well with winter vegetables such as cauliflower florets or carrot slices instead of spinach. These add a particularly delicious flavour.

Melt half the butter in a saucepan, add the millet and fry for about 5 minutes, stirring. Add the boiling water and cook for about 20 minutes or till the water is absorbed. Set aside.

Melt the remaining butter in a large frying pan and add the onions with a little water. Cover and braise over moderate heat for about 10 minutes, stirring occasionally, till the onions become translucent. Uncover, add the spinach and continue cooking for a few more minutes, stirring occasionally, till the spinach is wilted. Sprinkle with the flour, mix well and gradually add the warm milk, stirring so as not to form lumps. Salt to taste and add the nutmeg. Lower the flame, cover and cook for a further 10 minutes. Add the Parmesan and millet, mix well and reheat briefly, then transfer to a heated serving dish.
Serves 4.

Lettuce Rolls with Millet

INVOLTINI DI LATTUGA E MIGLIO

600ml / 1 pint / 2½ cups water
Salt
210g / 7oz / 1 cup millet,
carefully washed
12 large lettuce leaves
3 tbsp extra virgin olive oil
210g / 7oz lettuce, finely
shredded
120g / 4oz / ½ cup ricotta cheese
1 tbsp fresh thyme leaves

A superb and different way to serve millet. Try it also using cabbage instead of lettuce leaves.

Put the water in a large saucepan, add salt to taste and bring to the boil. Add the millet and cook over a very low flame for about 20 minutes or until the water has been absorbed. Remove from the heat.

Meanwhile, blanch the lettuce leaves in boiling water, one at a time, for 1 minute, then remove gently so as not to tear them. Dip briefly in cold water and lay to dry on a kitchen towel.

Put the oil in a frying pan over moderate heat. When hot, add the shredded lettuce. Cook for a couple of minutes, stirring, until the lettuce has wilted. Add the millet and continue stirring over the heat for a few more minutes. Remove from the heat. Add the ricotta and thyme, mixing well.

Divide the millet mixture into 12 portions. Place one in the centre of each lettuce leaf, tuck in the sides and roll up into a parcel. Place on a steamer rack over boiling water and steam for 5 minutes. Transfer to a serving dish and serve.
Serves 4.

Carrot and Oat Pudding

TORTA DI CAROTE ALL' AVENA

300g / 10oz carrots, grated
60g / 2oz / ⅓ cup oatflakes
(old-fashioned oats)
90g / 3oz / 6 tbsp butter
2 tbsp milk
2 eggs (US large)
120g / 4oz / ¾ cup plain flour
(all-purpose flour)
1 tbsp fresh oregano
20g / ¾oz / ½ tsp baking powder
Salt and pepper

This is very high in vitamin A and calcium, as well as being mouthwatering.

Preheat the oven to 180°C / 350°F / Gas 4.
Cook the grated carrots and oatflakes (oats) in the butter over moderate heat for about 10 minutes, stirring often. Allow to cool.
Warm the milk in a small saucepan.
Using a food processor, blend the eggs with the flour, oregano, milk, baking powder and seasoning till you have a smooth batter. Add to the carrots and mix.
Grease a baking dish with butter and pour in the mixture. Bake for about half an hour until firm. Serve hot. *Serves 4.*

Oat, Carrot, Celery and Radish Salad

**AVENA CRUDA, CAROTE, SEDANO
E RAPANELLI**

150g / 5oz / 1½ cups oatflakes
(old-fashioned oats), soaked in
water for 24 hours and drained
1 carrot, grated
1 celery stalk, grated
A few radishes, grated
1 baby onion (pearl onion),
finely chopped
3 tbsp chopped fresh flat-leaf
Italian parsley
120g / 4oz Emmenthal cheese,
cut into little cubes
1 tbsp capers, chopped
Salt
Juice of 1 lemon
4 tbsp extra virgin olive oil

Here's a very healthy recipe, hailing from the whole-food tradition of the Dolomites, one of the most beautiful Alpine regions of North Italy.

Rinse the oats well and place in a bowl. Mix with the carrot, celery, radishes, onion, parsley, Emmenthal and capers.

Dissolve a little salt in the lemon juice in a small bowl. Add the oil. Pour over the vegetables, toss and serve. *Serves 4.*

Carrot and Oat Pudding

Semolina Roll with Peas and Artichokes

ROTOLO DI SEMOLINO PISELLI E CARCIOFI

4 small globe artichokes
Juice of ½ lemon
120g / 4oz / 1 cup shelled fresh green peas
30g / 1oz / 2 tbsp butter
4 tbsp chopped fresh flat-leaf Italian parsley
5 tbsp water
1 litre / 1¾ pints / 1 US quart milk
240g / 8oz / 1⅓ cups semolina (farina)
2 eggs
120g / 4oz Emmenthal cheese, thinly sliced
Salt and pepper

Semolina is obtained by grinding different grains together. It is frequently used in soups and creams, and as the base for the famous Gnocchi alla Romana. This way of preparing it is attractive and not particularly hard to do. For an even simpler preparation, pour the semolina mixture into a buttered baking dish, arrange the peas, cheese and artichokes on top, then bake until the top is lightly browned.

Remove the hairy chokes from the artichokes and remove the tough outer leaves. Slice thinly and put into water to which the lemon juice has been added.

Cook the peas in a little boiling water for about 10 minutes. Drain and set aside.

Drain the artichokes and pat dry. Heat the butter in a large frying pan and add the drained artichokes and half the parsley. Add the water and cook over a low flame for about 10 minutes. Stir occasionally. Drain, saving the cooking liquid, and keep warm.

Warm the milk in a saucepan and pour in the semolina in a thin stream, stirring. Cook over a low flame for about 15 minutes, stirring occasionally with a wooden spoon to avoid lumps. Turn off the heat, then add the the eggs one by one, mixing well. Remove from the heat at once.

Preheat the oven to 220°C / 425°F / Gas 7.

Dampen a kitchen towel. Pour the semolina mixture on to it and, using a spatula, spread to a rectangle about 1cm / ½ inch thick. Arrange the peas, cheese and artichokes on it. Season to taste. Using the towel to lift it, roll up the semolina rectangle like a Swiss roll (jelly roll).

Transfer the roll to a buttered baking dish and moisten with the cooking liquid from the artichokes.

Bake for about 20 minutes.

Remove from oven and leave to rest for a minute. Cut into 1cm / ½ inch slices, arrange on a warm serving dish and serve. *Serves 4.*

Semolina Roll with Peas and Artichokes

Barley with Artichokes

ORZO E CARCIOFI

*210g / 7oz / 1 cup pearl barley,
carefully washed and soaked
overnight in 750ml /
1¼ pints / 3 cups water
4 globe artichokes, cleaned,
sliced and left to soak in water
acidulated with a little lemon
juice
2 tbsp extra virgin olive oil
2 garlic cloves, chopped
210g / 7oz potatoes, peeled and
diced
Salt and pepper
3 tbsp chopped fresh flat-leaf
Italian parsley*

Preceded by a soup and followed by a light salad, this forms the heart of a tasty complete meal.

Cook the barley in its soaking water: bring to a boil and simmer over high heat for 10 minutes, then lower the heat, cover and cook for a further 40-50 minutes or until all the water is absorbed. Remove from the heat and set aside.

Drain the artichokes and pat dry. Heat the oil in a saucepan, add the garlic, drained artichokes and potatoes and fry over high heat for a few minutes, stirring often. Season to taste, cover and keep cooking over a low flame until the vegetables are tender, adding a little water to keep them moist.

Add the barley and parsley and cook for a few more minutes, stirring well. Transfer to a warmed serving dish and serve. *Serves 4.*

Barley Salad

ORZO IN INSALATA

*210g / 7oz / 1 cup pearl barley,
washed well and soaked
overnight in 750ml / 1¼ pints /
3 cups water
Salt
1 red sweet (bell) pepper, diced
1 yellow sweet (bell) pepper,
diced
8 cherry tomatoes, halved
1 small onion, sliced
2 tbsp fresh marjoram leaves
12 pitted black Kalamata olives
120g / 4oz goat's cheese, diced
2 tbsp vinegar
4 tbsp extra virgin olive oil*

The barley for this salad can be cooked the preceding day and kept in the refrigerator until it is time to dress and serve it.

Drain the barley, reserving the soaking water. Pour the water into a saucepan and bring to the boil. Dry the barley with a kitchen towel and place in a frying pan. Toast the barley, stirring, for 7-8 minutes or till it gives off a sweet smell. Add to the boiling water with salt to taste. Cook gently for about 50 minutes, covered. Remove from the heat and let it sit until all the water is absorbed. Leave to cool.

Transfer the barley to a bowl. Add the peppers, tomatoes, onion, marjoram, olives and cheese. Dissolve a little salt in the vinegar and add the oil. Pour over the barley salad and mix well. Let the flavours mingle for a few minutes, then serve. *Serves 4.*

Brown Rice Ring with Wild Mushrooms

ANELLO DI RISO INTEGRALE CON FUNGHI DI BOSCO

300g / 10oz / 1⅔ cups brown rice, carefully washed
1 litre / 1¾ pints / 1 US quart water
2 sprigs fresh rosemary
Salt
4 tbsp extra virgin olive oil
4 garlic cloves, chopped
450g / 1lb fresh wild mushrooms, washed and sliced
3 tbsp chopped fresh flat-leaf Italian parsley

The characteristic flavour of brown rice blends well with porcini mushrooms, though other types will do as well. The cooking time for rice can vary quite a bit depending on the variety, anything from 30 to 60 minutes. For the mushrooms, the rule is to cook them over high heat and remove when they begin to lose their liquid.

Place the rice, water, rosemary and a little salt in a saucepan over high heat. Bring to the boil and cook uncovered for about 10 minutes. Lower the flame, cover and cook for a further 40 minutes or so, without stirring, until the rice is tender. Discard the rosemary, remove from heat and leave covered for 10 minutes.

Generously oil a small ring mould, 15cm / 6 inches diameter. Press the rice into the mould and keep warm.

Heat the oil in a frying pan over a high flame, add the garlic and fry until it has a golden colour. Add the mushrooms and cook for about 10 minutes, stirring frequently. Remove from the heat, add the parsley and salt to taste, and stir well.

Turn out the rice ring on a warmed serving dish, place the mushrooms in the middle and serve. *Serves 4.*

Sprouted Buckwheat with Apples, Radishes and Emmenthal Cheese

GERMOGLI DI GRANO SARACENO CON MELE, RAPANELLI E EMMENTHAL

120g / 4oz sprouted buckwheat
2 apples, peeled, cored, diced and sprinkled with a little lemon juice
12 baby radishes, finely sliced
1 leek, cut lengthwise into thin strips
120g / 4oz Emmenthal cheese, diced
Juice of 1 lemon
1 tbsp paprika
4 tbsp extra virgin olive oil
Salt
A few lettuce leaves

When you sprout grains, it is on the third day that they attain their peak nutritional value. You can use a variety of grains, such as oats, rye, wheat or any other you please. To sprout grains, leave them to soak overnight in a little water, then lay them in a strainer, put in a dark place, and rinse at least twice a day in abundant running water.

Rinse the sprouts well and dry them a bit, then place in a bowl. Add the apples, radishes, leek and cheese.

Blend together the lemon juice, paprika, oil and a little salt in a bowl.

Pour this dressing over the salad, toss and let sit a few minutes.

Arrange lettuce leaves on the bottom of a serving dish. Put the salad on top and serve. *Serves 4.*

Rice with Lentils

RISO CON LENTICCHIE

*210g / 7oz / 1 cup brown rice,
carefully washed
750ml / 1¼ pints / 3 cups water
Salt and pepper
4 tbsp extra virgin olive oil
1 onion, sliced
150g / 5oz / ¾ cup lentils
2 tbsp tomato paste
1 garlic clove, chopped
1 tbsp chopped fresh flat-leaf
Italian parsley*

A balanced dish containing many necessary nutrients. I suggest
accompanying it with Chicory (Belgian Endive), Orange and Radicchio Salad
(page 122) and Cauliflower with Breadcrumbs (page 128).

Put the rice and water in a saucepan and bring to the boil. Cook for 10 minutes over high heat, then add a little salt. Cover and cook for 40 minutes over a low flame, till the water is absorbed and the rice is tender. Set aside, still covered.

Put half the oil in a saucepan and fry the onion over high heat until soft. Add the lentils and twice their volume of water. Stir in the tomato paste, season to taste and cook for about 20 minutes or until the liquid has been absorbed.

Mix the remaining oil with the garlic, parsley and a pinch of salt.

Transfer the rice and lentils to a bowl add the dressing and toss well. Serve warm. *Serves 4.*

Warm Steamed Sweet Corn Salad

INSALATA TIEPIDA DI MAIS

*4 ears sweet corn
1 small cauliflower, cut into
little florets
2 courgettes (zucchini), cut into
little cubes
120g / 4oz / 1 cup shelled fresh
green peas
4 tbsp extra virgin olive oil
Juice of 1 lemon
Salt and pepper
A few fresh basil leaves, torn*

Here's a light second course, perfect after a hearty opener like Gemelli with
Garlic and Mushrooms (page 73).

Cook the sweet corn in plenty of boiling salted water for about 15 minutes or until tender. Drain. When cool enough to handle, cut the kernels from the cobs.

Steam the cauliflower florets, courgettes (zucchini), peas and sweet corn kernels for about 15 minutes. Leave to cool for a few minutes.

Mix together the oil, lemon juice and some salt and pepper in a small bowl. Transfer the vegetables to a salad bowl. Sprinkle with the basil and dressing, mix gently and serve. *Serves 4.*

Bread and Tomato Salad

PANZANELLA

450g/1lb stale coarse-textured whole wheat bread, cut into pieces

250ml/8fl oz/1 cup red wine vinegar

2 tomatoes, not too ripe, sliced

3 red onions, finely sliced

2 cucumbers, peeled and sliced

2 celery stalks, sliced

A few radishes, sliced

12 olives

12 fresh basil leaves, shredded by hand

Salt and pepper

6 tbsp extra virgin olive oil

We call this typical Tuscan dish *Panzanella*. To have it come out perfectly the bread must be made without salt and be really dry. The original version is made only with bread, tomatoes, onion and oil. These days it is often enriched with cucumbers, olives, celery or radishes, as here.

Place the stale bread chunks in a bowl, cover with water and the vinegar and leave to soak until soft. Drain and squeeze out as much liquid as possible. Transfer to a large bowl. Add the tomatoes, onions, cucumbers, celery, radishes, olives and basil. Stir delicately. Season to taste, pour over the oil and mix a little more, then serve immediately. *Serves 4.*

VEGETABLE AND GRAIN

side dishes

This chapter includes vegetables as accompaniments and dishes made with dried beans, peas and lentils. These recipes are just the 'blueprints': almost every recipe can be made in exactly the same way substituting other vegetables or pulses (legumes). For example, if you're making a raw salad in the middle of winter and are having difficulty in finding some of the vegetables listed, experiment with whatever is available – red chicory or radicchio, for example, with its distinctive bitter taste, is usually available in winter and makes a delicious and nourishing alternative to the usual summer salad fare.

Generally my rule of thumb when composing summer salads is not to put more than three types of vegetables together; any more than three and I find the different flavours will tend to cancel each other out, resulting in confusion instead of clear and distinctly separate flavours.

However, when the seasons change, our ways of preparing vegetables also change. When the weather cools I also add some cooked vegetables to my salads. For instance, to a salad of lettuce, very finely sliced carrots, radicchio and rocket (arugula) I might add steamed

beetroot (beets) or potatoes, Brussels sprouts or cauliflower. The mixture of cooked and raw vegetables is very pleasing.

Dried beans, peas and lentils play a very important role in vegetarian cuisine, providing a complete protein when served in conjunction with cereal grains. Together with vegetables they complete the necessary amino acid quotient, to give us high-quality protein in perfect balance with carbohydrates, fibre, vitamins and trace minerals. As they are so highly nourishing, it is necessary only to consume small quantities.

Pulses, or legumes, keep very well in their dry state and are very easy to prepare. Soaking them overnight is the hardest part to organize; once they're cooking it's almost impossible to go wrong, and in this chapter you will find all the necessary instructions. Once cooked, pulses (legumes) keep very well in the refrigerator for a few days, and can be frozen. For speed and convenience, canned beans can be used.

Artichokes with Lemon Dip

CARCIOFI CON SALSA DI LIMONE

Juice of 1 lemon
6 young globe artichokes, about
150g / 5oz each
3 tbsp chopped fresh flat-leaf
Italian parsley
10 green olives, sliced
1 hard-boiled egg, chopped
6 tbsp extra virgin olive oil
Salt and pepper

When in season, artichokes are so tasty that they can be eaten raw, simply dipped in good extra virgin olive oil and salt.

Fill a bowl with water and add 1 tbsp lemon juice. Prepare the artichokes: cut off all but 2.5cm / 1 inch of the stalk and remove the outer leaves until you arrive at the tender parts. Cut the artichokes in half lengthwise. Remove the hairy chokes. As they are prepared, put the artichokes in the bowl of lemon water.

Combine the remaining lemon juice with the parsley, olives, egg, oil and seasoning in a small serving bowl. Mix well. Put the bowl in the centre of a large serving dish.
Drain the artichokes and dry well with paper towels. Arrange on the platter around the lemon dip.
Serves 4.

Carrots with Balsamic Vinegar Sauce

CAROTE AL BALSAMICO

2 tbsp extra virgin olive oil
450g / 1lb carrots, cut into
strips 1 × 3cm / ½ × 1½ inches
2 juniper berries, crushed
4 tbsp balsamic vinegar
1 tbsp caraway seeds
Salt

The sweet taste of carrots is accentuated by this very flavourful sauce. Sautéed carrots make a wonderful partner for grains, eggs and other vegetables, such as potatoes.

Heat the oil in a large frying pan over moderate heat. When the oil takes on a more liquid appearance add the carrots and juniper berries, stirring well. Cook for about 20 minutes, stirring frequently. Add a little water if necessary to keep from burning.
Add the balsamic vinegar and caraway seeds.

Lower the heat and continue cooking for a few more minutes or till the sauce has thickened a little. Remove from the heat, add a pinch of salt, cover and let sit for a few minutes.
Transfer to a warmed serving platter and serve. *Serves 4.*

Artichokes with Lemon Dip

Pepper, Onion and Tomato Salad

PEPERONI, POMODORI E CIPOLLE

4 green sweet (bell) peppers
4 tomatoes
2 white onions, sliced and
separated into rings
2 gherkins, sliced crosswise
2 tbsp red wine vinegar
Salt and pepper
4 tbsp extra virgin olive oil

This salad makes a colourful accompaniment to the bread salad on page 111,
reinforcing its flavours.

Roast the peppers over an open flame or under the grill (broiler) until charred on all sides. Wrap in a plastic bag and cool, then peel. Remove the seeds and cut into thin strips. Drop the tomatoes into a pan of boiling water and blanch for a minute. Drain and peel. Remove the seeds and cut into small cubes. Drop the onion rings into boiling water and blanch for a few seconds, then drain and place on paper towels to dry.

Arrange the gherkins in the centre of a serving dish. Surround with pepper strips, then onion rings, then tomatoes.

Mix the vinegar with seasoning to taste in a small bowl. Add the oil, mix well and pour over the salad. Serve at once. *Serves 4.*

Radicchio with Mint

RADICCHIO ALLA MENTA

300g / 10oz green or red
radicchio, finely shredded
Handful of fresh mint leaves
1 tbsp honey
1 garlic clove, crushed in a
garlic press
4 tbsp balsamic vinegar
Salt
4 tbsp extra virgin olive oil

This sweet and sour dressing makes a perfect complement to the powerful,
slightly bitter flavour of radicchio.

Put the radicchio and mint leaves in a salad bowl.

In a small bowl stir together the honey, garlic, balsamic vinegar and a pinch of salt. Add the olive oil and set aside for a few minutes to let the flavours mingle.

Stir the dressing briskly, then pour on to the salad. Toss well and serve. *Serves 4.*

Celery and Parmesan Salad

SEDANO E PARMIGIANO

300g / 10oz celery, very thinly
sliced
180g / 6oz Parmesan cheese,
grated into little flakes
2 tbsp balsamic vinegar
4 tbsp extra virgin olive oil
Salt and pepper

Parmesan cheese combines happily with many vegetables, so you might try
substituting sliced raw fennel or artichokes for the celery.

Place a layer of celery in the bottom of a serving dish. Cover with a layer of Parmesan flakes, spreading evenly.

In a small bowl, mix the vinegar, oil and a little salt. Pour this dressing over the salad. Sprinkle with pepper and serve. *Serves 4.*

Cress (Watercress), Apple and Celery Salad

GERMOGLI, MELE E SEDANO

*2 apples, peeled, cut into small
cubes and sprinkled with a
little lemon juice
5 celery stalks, thinly sliced
60g / 2oz / ½ cup walnuts,
roughly chopped
½ tbsp caraway seeds
120g / 4oz / 1 cup fresh mustard
and cress (watercress)
Juice of 1 lemon
Salt and pepper
4 tbsp extra virgin olive oil*

This is a crunchy and appetizing salad that makes a perfect accompaniment to a dish such as Onion, Egg and Potato Cake (page 94). Use other types of sprouts if you like, such as mung bean, fenugreek, alfalfa, etc.

Combine the apples, celery, walnuts, caraway seeds and cress (watercress) in a salad bowl. In a small bowl mix together the lemon juice and a little salt and pepper. Add the oil. Pour on to the salad, toss and serve. *Serves 4.*

Iced Tomatoes

POMODORI GHIACCIATI

*210g / 7oz tomatoes, cut into
wedges
2 tbsp dried oregano
3 tbsp balsamic vinegar
Salt and pepper
4 tbsp extra virgin olive oil
8 ice cubes*

A very simple, easy salad, this is perfect for sweltering summer days.
It requires top-quality tomatoes, solid and sun-ripened.
It's better not to refrigerate them before use, as this robs them of some
of their delicious fragrance.

Place the tomatoes in a salad bowl. Dress with the oregano, vinegar, and some salt and pepper. Mix well. Add the oil and mix again.

Scatter the ice cubes over the salad. Let sit a few minutes so the ice cools the tomatoes. Serve before the ice begins to melt. *Serves 4.*

Overleaf: Cress (Watercress), Apple and Celery Salad, Iced Tomatoes

Lemon, Fennel and Rocket (Arugula) Salad

FINOCCHI E RUCOLA

2 lemons
2 fennel bulbs, thinly sliced
crosswise
120g / 4oz rocket (arugula),
stems removed and shredded
Salt
4 tbsp extra virgin olive oil

This salad is ideal summer fare, although it is delicious with very spicy dishes at any time of year. Omit the fennel, if you prefer.

Peel the lemons, carefully removing all the white pith. Slice into thin strips and discard any seeds. Combine with the fennel and rocket (arugula) in a bowl. Dress with a pinch of salt and the oil. Mix well. Leave to sit for a few minutes to blend the flavours, then serve.
Serves 4.

Carrot, Rocket (Arugula) and Olive Salad

CAROTE ALLE OLIVE

450g / 1lb carrots, grated
100g / 3½oz rocket (arugula)
Salt
1 tbsp white wine vinegar
2 tbsp extra virgin olive oil
120g / 4oz / ⅔ cup black olives,
sliced
1 tbsp fresh oregano

Why not serve this with Carrot and Oat Pudding (page 104) for harmony of colour and a good dose of vitamin A?

Combine the grated carrots and rocket (arugula) in a salad bowl. Blend a pinch of salt with the vinegar in a small bowl. Mix in the oil. Pour over the salad and toss. Sprinkle with the olives and oregano and serve at once. *Serves 4.*

Beetroot (Beets) Salad with Young Spinach

BARBABIETOLE, SESAMO E SPINACI

2 tbsp extra virgin olive oil
Juice of 1 lemon
Salt and pepper
2 tbsp sesame seeds
4 tbsp raisins, soaked to soften
300g / 10oz fresh young spinach
leaves
350g / 12oz beetroot (beets),
cooked, peeled and cut into
small cubes

To eat raw in salad, spinach leaves must be very young and tender. To obtain enough leaves with these characteristics for this salad, you need to buy at least 1kg / 2lb. The left-over leaves can be used to make Onions Stuffed with Spinach (page 100).

Blend together the oil, lemon juice and some seasoning in a small bowl. Add the sesame seeds and raisins and leave for about 10 minutes to allow the flavours to mingle.
Place the spinach in a bowl. Add half of the dressing and toss. Put the beetroot (beets) in another bowl. Add the remaining dressing and stir. Arrange the spinach in a ring on a serving dish and place the beetroot (beets) in the centre. Serve. *Serves 4.*

Lemon, Fennel and Rocket (Arugula) Salad

Asparagus with Warm Bread Sauce

ASPARAGI IN SALSA DI PANE

900g / 2lb asparagus
60g / 2oz crustless coarse-textured whole wheat bread, about two slices
4 tbsp white wine vinegar
1 hard-boiled egg
60g / 2oz fresh flat-leaf Italian parsley
60g / 2oz / 1⁄3 cup capers
4 tbsp extra virgin olive oil
Salt and pepper

This is an elegant way to serve asparagus.

Steam the asparagus until tender. Keep warm. Moisten the bread with half of the vinegar and squeeze dry. Roughly chop together the egg, parsley, capers and bread. Place the remaining vinegar, the oil and seasoning in a small saucepan. Heat over a low flame until warm. Add the bread mixture. Arrange the asparagus on a heated serving dish, dress with the sauce and serve. *Serves 4.*

Peas with Paprika

PISELLI ALLA PAPRICA

600g / 1 1⁄4lb / 4 cups shelled fresh green peas
4 tbsp single cream (light cream)
1 small onion, thinly sliced
1 tsp paprika
Salt

This is a sweet and spicy dish. It makes an excellent accompaniment to Polenta with Leeks (page 79).

Steam the peas for about 20 minutes until tender.
Heat the cream in a saucepan, add the onion and cook over low heat for about 7 minutes. Add the peas, paprika and salt to taste and let the flavours mingle for a few minutes. Transfer to a heated serving dish and serve. *Serves 4.*

Chicory (Belgian Endive), Orange and Radicchio Salad

INDIVIA, ARANCE E RADICCHIO ROSSO

2 oranges, very thinly sliced (unpeeled)
2 chicory (Belgian endive), finely shredded
1 radicchio heart, finely shredded
120g / 4oz young lettuce leaves, shredded
Juice of 1 orange
2 tbsp balsamic vinegar
Salt and pepper
4 tbsp extra virgin olive oil
2 tbsp sesame seeds

The use of oranges to enhance vegetable salads is quite common in Sicily, where the orange groves are unforgettably beautiful. The peel is left on the oranges in this recipe, so seek out organically grown produce and slice them as thin as you can.

Cut the orange slices into wedges. Mix with the chicory (endive), radicchio and lettuce. Strain the orange juice into a small bowl and add the balsamic vinegar and seasoning. Stir, then add the oil and sesame seeds. Dress the salad, toss well and serve. *Serves 4.*

Asparagus with Warm Bread Sauce

Baked Courgettes (Zucchini)

ZUCCHINE AL FORNO

4 medium courgettes (zucchini)
30g / 1oz / ¼ cup freshly grated
Parmesan cheese
¼ tsp grated nutmeg
Salt and pepper
1 egg white (US large)

Very delicate, this dish works well any time of year. Serve with a grain dish.

Preheat the oven to 180° / C350°F / Gas 4. Blanch the courgettes (zucchini) in boiling salted water for a few minutes. Drain. Trim the ends and cut the courgettes (zucchini) in half lengthwise. Scrape out at least half of the inside pulp and put it in a food processor with the Parmesan, nutmeg and seasoning. Process until smooth. Beat the egg white into a stiff peak. Fold into the stuffing.

Fill the courgette (zucchini) shells generously with the stuffing. Grease a baking dish with oil and arrange the stuffed courgettes (zucchini) in it. Bake for about 40 minutes or until the stuffing has risen and is golden brown. Add a few tablespoons of water to the dish occasionally if necessary.
Transfer to a heated serving dish and serve immediately. *Serves 4.*

Broad Beans (Fava Beans) with Spring Onions (Scallions) and Pecorino

FAVE, CIPOLLOTTI E PECORINO

A few lettuce leaves
900g / 2lb fresh young broad
beans (fava beans), shelled
2 spring onions (scallions), cut
into thin strips
210g / 7oz aged pecorino cheese,
shaved into flakes
Salt and pepper
4 tbsp extra virgin olive oil

There's nothing like fresh broad (fava) beans to evoke the freshness of spring.
To enjoy them at their very simplest, we serve them in their shells in a big bowl in the centre of the table, with slices of fresh pecorino served alongside.

Use the lettuce leaves to line a salad bowl. Mix the beans with the spring onions and place them on the lettuce leaves. Sprinkle on the pecorino flakes.

Combine salt to taste, a generous grating of pepper and the oil. Stir well with a fork, pour over the salad and mix well. Serve.
Serves 4.

Broad Beans (Fava Beans) with Spring Onions and Pecorino

Little Chicory (Belgian Endive) Boats with Beans

BARCHETTE DI INDIVIA AI FAGIOLI

Here's an original and entertaining way to serve these ingredients. Try it as an appetizer.

120g / 4oz / ⅔ cup dried cannellini beans or other white beans, soaked overnight and drained
Salt and pepper
4 tbsp extra virgin olive oil
8 tsp red wine vinegar
2 heads chicory (Belgian endive)
Bunch of fresh flat-leaf Italian parsley, chopped

Rinse the beans, place in a saucepan and add water to come 2.5cm / 1 inch above the beans. Bring to the boil and simmer for 1½ hours or until the beans are tender. Salt to taste towards the end of the cooking.

Drain the beans and purée in a food mill. Place the purée in a bowl and season with the oil, vinegar, salt and pepper. Stir well.

Take the chicory leaves one by one and fill with a generous spoonful of the bean mixture. Arrange the filled leaves on a serving dish, garnish with a sprinkling of parsley and serve.

Serves 4.

Frisée (Curly Endive) Ripassata

CICORIA RIPASSATA

Like all bitter vegetables, frisée (endive) stimulates the liver and digestive organs. You can also make this dish using extra virgin olive oil and hot chili pepper instead of butter and nutmeg.

900g / 2lb frisée (curly endive), shredded
Juice of 1 lemon
60g / 2oz / 4 tbsp butter
Pinch of grated nutmeg
Salt and pepper

Cook the frisée (endive) in boiling water with 1 tsp lemon juice for about 10 minutes or until tender. Drain and squeeze dry.

Melt the butter in a large frying pan. Add the frisée (endive) and remaining lemon juice. Season with nutmeg, salt and pepper. Turn up the heat and cook for a couple of minutes, stirring often. Turn down the heat to low, cover and let the frisée (endive) absorb the flavours for about 10 more minutes.

Transfer to a serving dish and serve.

Serves 4.

Little Chicory (Belgian Endive) Boats with Beans

Baked Potatoes and Onion

PATATE E CIPOLLE GRATINATE

450g / 1lb potatoes, peeled and
cut into 2.5cm / 1 inch chunks
2 red onions, cut into 1cm/½
inch thick slices
6 tbsp extra virgin olive oil
2 tbsp fresh oregano
Salt

This makes a complementary side dish to something raw and crunchy, like
the Chicory (Belgian Endive), Orange and Radicchio Salad (see page 122).

Preheat the oven to 180°C / 350°F / Gas 4. Put the potato chunks and onion slices in a baking dish. Dress with the oil, oregano and a little salt. Bake for about 40 minutes or until browned, stirring once in a while. Transfer to a heated serving dish and serve. *Serves 4.*

Cauliflower with Breadcrumbs

CAVOLFIORE AI PANGRATTATO

600g / 1¼lb cauliflower florets
from 1 large cauliflower
4 tbsp extra virgin olive oil
1 small onion, thinly sliced
30g / 1oz / ¼ cup dry
breadcrumbs
3 tbsp chopped fresh flat-leaf
Italian parsley
Salt and pepper

For an alternative to the parsley, try using caraway seeds.

Steam the cauliflower florets until tender but still firm. Keep warm. Heat the oil in a frying pan, add the onion and soften over a lively flame, stirring often. Add the breadcrumbs and fry until crisp, stirring often. Add the cauliflower and stir. Sprinkle with the parsley and salt and pepper to taste. Stir again, then transfer to a heated serving dish. Serve immediately. *Serves 4.*

Peas with Lettuce

PISELLI E LATTUGA

60g / 2oz / 4 tbsp butter
1 white onion, thinly sliced
2 lettuce hearts, shredded
600g / 1¼lb / 4 cups shelled fresh
green peas
125ml / 4fl oz / ½ cup water
1 tbsp sugar
Bunch of fresh tarragon
Salt and pepper
2 tbsp double cream (heavy
cream)

This is a typical springtime dish that complements many main courses.

Combine the butter, onion, lettuce and peas in a saucepan over moderate heat. Stirring often, cook for 5-6 minutes. Add the water, sugar, tarragon and seasoning to taste and cover. Lower the heat and cook for about half an hour or until the peas are tender. Remove the lid and reduce the liquid. Discard the tarragon. Add the cream, mix well and transfer to a warmed serving dish. Serve immediately. *Serves 4.*

Green Beans with Mint Sauce

FAGIOLINI IN SALSA DI MENTA

700g / 1½lb green beans
2 tbsp extra virgin olive oil
1 garlic clove, chopped
1 tbsp vinegar
2 tbsp chopped fresh
mint leaves
Salt

Fresh and festive, this makes an excellent accompaniment to the barley salad on page 108.

Cook the green beans in plenty of boiling salted water for 5 minutes or till tender but still firm. Drain. Arrange in a warmed serving dish.

Meanwhile, when the beans are almost done, start heating the oil in a frying pan. Add the garlic and fry over high heat for a couple of minutes. Add the vinegar, mint and a pinch of salt. Heat, then pour over the green beans and serve immediately. *Serves 4.*

Green Beans with Lemon Sauce

FAGIOLINI IN SALSA DI LIMONE

700g / 1½lb green beans
60g / 2oz / 4 tbsp butter
1 tsp flour
1 egg yolk
Juice of 1 lemon
3 tbsp dry white wine
Salt
1 tbsp chopped fresh basil

Cook the green beans in plenty of boiling salted water until just tender but still crisp, about 5 minutes. Drain and cool under cold running water. Cut into 2.5cm / 1 inch diagonal lengths. Place in a frying pan.

Whisk together the butter, flour, egg yolk, lemon juice and wine. Pour over the green beans, set on moderate heat and cook until thickened, stirring with a wooden spoon. Do not boil. Stir in salt to taste, then transfer to a warm serving platter. Sprinkle with the basil and serve. *Serves 4.*

Broad Beans (Fava Beans) with Fennel and Apples

FAVE, FINOCCHI E MELE

30g / 1oz / 2 tbsp butter
700g / 1½lb fresh young broad
beans (fava beans), shelled
1 fennel bulb, thinly sliced
1 apple, peeled, cored and diced
Salt and pepper

This dish combines very delicate, subtle flavours, and is an ideal accompaniment to fresh creamy cheeses such as ricotta or cottage cheese.

Heat the butter in a frying pan over moderate heat, add the beans and a little water and stew, covered, for about 20 minutes. Add the fennel and apple and continue cooking, covered, for 10 minutes. Then cook uncovered to reduce excess liquid. Season to taste. Transfer to a serving dish and serve. *Serves 4.*

Chick Peas with Onion

CECI E CIPOLLE

300g/10oz/1½ cups dried chick peas, soaked overnight and drained
Salt
2 onions, peeled
2 tbsp balsamic vinegar
1 tsp chopped fresh rosemary
4 tbsp extra virgin olive oil

If you want to make this dish even tastier, sauté the slices of steamed onion in a few tablespoons of extra virgin olive oil.

Rinse the chick peas and place in a saucepan. Cover with cold water and simmer for about 2 hours or until tender. Salt to taste towards the end. Drain and place in a salad bowl. Mash the chick peas a little with a fork.

Meanwhile, steam the onions whole until tender, about 30 minutes. Slice and add to the chick peas. Mix together the vinegar, rosemary, oil and some salt in a bowl. Pour over the chick peas, stir well and serve. *Serves 4.*

Creamed Beans with Carrots

CREMA DI FAGIOLI CON CAROTE

210g/7oz/1 cup dried cannellini beans or other white beans, soaked overnight and drained
Large bunch of fresh sage
Salt
4 tbsp extra virgin olive oil
Juice of 1 lemon
4 carrots, cut into strips lengthwise
Paprika

This dish has the advantage of keeping well in the refrigerator. In hot weather it is also delicious served cold.

Rinse the beans, place in a saucepan and add water to come 2.5cm/1 inch above the beans. Bring to the boil, add the sage and simmer for 1½ hours or until the beans are tender. Add salt to taste towards the end.
Drain the beans, discard the sage and pass through a food mill. Pour the purée into a serving bowl. Add the oil and lemon juice and mix well. Arrange the carrot sticks in a ring around the edge. Sprinkle with paprika and serve. *Serves 4.*

Beans with Tomato

FAGIOLI AL POMODORO

210g/7oz/1 cup dried cannellini beans, soaked overnight and drained
4 tbsp extra virgin olive oil
2 garlic cloves, chopped
A few fresh basil leaves
210g/7oz ripe plum tomatoes, peeled and diced (or use canned)
Salt and pepper

In winter, when basil is impossible to find, sage makes a successful alternative.

Rinse the beans, place in a saucepan and add water to come 2.5cm/1 inch above the beans. Bring to the boil and simmer for 1½ hours or until tender. Drain.
Heat the oil in a frying pan, add the garlic and basil and cook for a few minutes over moderate heat. Add the tomatoes and drained beans. Season to taste, cover and cook for a further 10 minutes over low heat. There should be some liquid left. Transfer to a heated serving dish and serve. *Serves 4.*

Green Beans with Tomato

FAGIOLINI AL POMODORO

A summer favourite.

2 tbsp extra virgin olive oil
210g / 7oz / 1 cup peeled, seeded
and chopped tomatoes,
well-drained
700g / 1½lb green beans, cut
into 2.5cm / 1 inch lengths
8 fresh basil leaves, shredded,
plus a few whole leaves to
garnish
Salt and pepper

Heat the oil in a frying pan, add the tomatoes and cook for about 10 minutes. Add the green beans and a few tablespoons of water. Simmer for about 15 minutes, stirring occasionally, till the green beans are tender. Add the shredded basil and mix. Season to taste. Transfer to a heated serving dish, garnish with whole basil leaves and serve. *Serves 4.*

Chick Pea Purée with Tomatoes

PASSATO DI CECI CON POMODORO

With some bread and cheese this dish could be a meal in itself, or it could follow a hearty soup.

300g / 10oz / 1½ cups dried chick
peas, soaked overnight and
drained
Salt and pepper
2 tbsp extra virgin olive oil
1 onion, sliced
2 garlic cloves, chopped
300g / 10oz ripe plum tomatoes,
peeled and diced (or use
canned)

Rinse the chick peas, place in a saucepan and cover with cold water. Simmer for 2 hours or until tender, adding salt to taste towards the end. Drain and purée, using a food mill.
Heat the oil in a frying pan over high heat. Add the onion and garlic and fry for about 5 minutes. Add the tomatoes and cook for another few minutes. Add the chick pea purée and pepper to taste, lower the flame and, stirring with a wooden spoon, continue cooking till the mixture is hot and has the right consistency – dry but creamy. Transfer to a heated serving dish and serve. *Serves 4.*

Chick Pea and Pepper Salad

CECI E PEPERONI

If you want to vary the taste of this salad, you can substitute basil leaves or Italian flat-leaf parsley for the tarragon.

300g / 10oz / 1½ cups dried chick
peas, soaked overnight and
drained
Salt and pepper
1 yellow sweet (bell) pepper,
1 green sweet (bell) pepper, and
1 red sweet (bell) pepper, diced
Juice of ½ lemon
4 tbsp extra virgin olive oil
2 tbsp chopped fresh tarragon

Rinse the chick peas, place in a saucepan and cover with cold water. Simmer for about 2 hours or until tender, adding salt to taste towards the end. Drain the chick peas and place in a salad bowl. Add the diced peppers. Mix together the lemon juice, oil, tarragon and seasoning in a small bowl. Pour over the chick peas, mix well and serve. *Serves 4.*

Lentils with Saffron

LENTICCHIE ALLO ZAFFERANO

2 tbsp extra virgin olive oil
2 bay leaves
½ onion, thinly sliced
300g / 10oz / 1½ cups red or
brown lentils, carefully washed
4 tbsp dry white wine
600ml / 1 pint / 2½ cups water
Pinch of saffron
Salt and pepper

For this type of recipe I advise you to use the tiny mountain lentils
(small red lentils) that need no presoaking and cook in about 20 minutes.
Always use twice as much water as lentils.

Heat the oil in a saucepan over moderate heat, add the bay leaves and onion and cook until the onion is translucent. Add the lentils and white wine, raise the heat and boil to evaporate the wine, stirring. Add the water and cook for about 15 minutes, covered. Dissolve the saffron in a little water and add it to the lentils. Season to taste. Finish cooking uncovered to evaporate excess liquid. Remove the bay leaves and serve. *Serves 4.*

Spicy Lentils with Tomato

LENTICCHIE AL POMODORO PICCANTE

2 tbsp extra virgin olive oil
2 garlic cloves, chopped
1 celery stalk, chopped
1 small carrot, chopped
2 bay leaves
300g / 10oz / 1½ cups lentils,
washed
300g / 10oz / 1½ cups canned
tomatoes, drained and diced
375ml / 12fl oz / 1½ cups water
Pinch of cayenne pepper
2 tbsp chopped fresh flat-leaf
Italian parsley
Salt

If you are using large green lentils for this recipe, it is advisable to soak them
overnight. If you prefer to use the smaller red ones, they need less cooking
time than specified in the recipe.

Heat the oil in a saucepan over moderate heat and add the garlic, celery, carrot and bay leaves. Fry for about 10 minutes. Add the lentils, tomatoes, water and cayenne pepper. Cook for about 1 hour or until the juices are absorbed and the lentils are tender. Add the parsley and salt to taste and transfer to a heated serving dish. *Serves 4.*

Lentils with Saffron

desserts

At home we enjoy making desserts but only in moderation. We, like many other Italians, tend to concentrate on first and main courses rather than on sweet things. Those desserts we do make are usually fairly simple and healthy, making the most of the delicate flavours of fresh seasonal fruits. Particular favourites of mine are Ricotta Pots with Raspberries, Stewed Apples with Saffron and Chestnut Montebianco.

If I want to make something really indulgent, I would choose Chocolate Cake; the version I give on page 143 is very rich and should keep you from craving chocolate for quite a while! Another special dessert is Fried Semolina Diamonds – flour and water dough which is dipped in sugar and then fried. These fritters are usually associated with Carnival, when their delicious cooking smells permeate the streets of Tuscany.

One of the most popular choices for dessert is ice cream, which can be flavoured with all kinds of seasonal fruits to make a refreshing and mouthwatering end to a meal. I like to serve ice cream in fruit shells. Tangerine ice cream or lemon sorbet, for example, can be scooped into the empty citrus shells before they are frozen for a last time, then served at the table to make a colourful and unusual presentation.

Stewed Apples with Saffron

MELE ALLO ZAFFERANO

60g / 2oz / 4 tbsp butter
4 apples, peeled and cut into
pieces
Pinch of saffron
1 tbsp sugar
4 tbsp water
Grated zest of ½ lemon

Here is a very easy recipe. It is pretty to look at too, with the intense yellow of the saffron. If you'd like it richer, decorate it with little dabs of whipped cream and sprinkle with chopped hazelnuts.

Melt the butter in a saucepan over high heat, add the apples and saffron and cook for a few minutes, stirring often. Add the sugar and water, lower the flame and cover. Cook until almost a purée, stirring occasionally. Add the lemon zest and cook for a few more minutes, then transfer to individual heated cups and serve immediately. *Serves 4.*

Raspberries in Syrup

LAMPONI SCIROPPATI

900g / 2lb / 4 cups raspberries
Juice of 1 lemon
300g / 10oz / 1⅓ cups caster
sugar (granulated sugar)
4 tbsp water

Here's a way to preserve summer fruit. It also works well with bilberries, blackberries, red currants or black currants. Always choose berries at their peak of maturity, free from blemishes, and clean them well without washing them. Try them with ice cream.

Place the berries in a large glass jar and sprinkle them with the lemon juice.
Dissolve the sugar with the water in a saucepan over low heat. Cook to a syrup that sticks to a wooden spoon. Pour over the berries. Seal the jar and sterilize by placing in a deep saucepan, covering with water and boiling for 20 minutes. Let cool, then remove from the water and store in a cool dark place. *Makes about 450g / 1lb / 2 cups.*

Sage Sorbet

SORBETTO ALLA SALVIA

210g / 7oz / 1 cup caster sugar
(granulated sugar)
500ml / 16fl oz / 2 cups water
175ml / 6fl oz / ¾ cup lemon
juice, strained
8-10 fresh sage leaves
2 egg whites

An herb sorbet is perfect to serve between courses of a particularly rich or spicy meal. The intriguing flavour will stimulate your guests' appetites.

Dissolve the sugar in the water in a saucepan, then boil for a few minutes. Add the strained lemon juice. Pour the mixture into a bowl and cool, then place in the freezer. When frozen, break into chunks and transfer to a food processor with the sage leaves and blend to a very fine cream. Beat the egg whites until stiff and fold delicately into the cream. Freeze again until softly set. *Serves 4-6.*

Ricotta Pots with Raspberries

TERRINA DI RICOTTA E LAMPONI

2 eggs, separated
3 tbsp caster sugar (granulated sugar)
3 tbsp chopped pistachio nuts
275g / 9oz / 1 cup plus 2 tbsp ricotta cheese
Grated zest and juice of ½ lemon
A little vanilla-flavoured caster sugar (granulated sugar)
450g / 1lb / 2 cups raspberries

It is important for this recipe that the raspberries be really sweet and ripe. For an alternative try wild strawberries, which are much more perfumed and flavourful than the cultivated ones. When in season, blackberries are also marvellous.

Preheat the oven to 200°C / 400°F / Gas 6. Beat the egg yolks with the sugar in a large bowl until pale and creamy. Add the pistachio nuts, ricotta, and lemon zest and juice. Beat the egg whites with the vanilla-flavoured sugar until stiff, then fold into the ricotta mixture.

Grease 4 little baking dishes or ramekins with butter. Divide the mixture among them and decorate with raspberries. Alternatively, bake in one large baking dish. Bake for about 20 minutes or until the tops have nicely browned. Serve immediately.
Serves 4.

Almond Biscuits

SPUMINI ALLE MANDORLE

3 egg whites
6 tbsp caster sugar (granulated sugar)
Pinch of salt
120g / 4oz / ¾ cup almonds, chopped

This recipe is complementary to the rice pudding recipe on page 139, in that it makes good use of the leftover egg whites.

Preheat the oven to 180°C / 350°F / Gas 4. Beat the egg whites with the sugar and salt till stiff. Fold in the almonds gently. Use a spoon to make little mounds of the mixture on

baking sheets lined with parchment paper. Bake for about 10 minutes. Turn off the heat and let the *spumini* cool slowly in the oven.
Makes about 30 biscuits.

Ricotta Pots with Raspberries, Almond Biscuits

Chestnut White Mountain

MONTEBIANCO DI CASTAGNE

500ml/16fl oz/2 cups whipping
cream (heavy cream)
120g/4oz/⅔ cup sugar
(granulated sugar)
450g/1lb chestnuts
250ml/8fl oz/1 cup milk
1 vanilla pod (vanilla bean),
split open
Salt

This is one of our most classical and best-loved midwinter desserts. Spectacular yet very simple to make, it requires a lot of patience for the shelling of the chestnuts. For this reason it is only made when someone in the family has the necessary time.

Whip the cream with 2 tbsp of the sugar. Put to chill in the refrigerator.

Remove the outer shells from the chestnuts. Make an incision in each one. Place them in a saucepan with sufficient water to cover and bring to the boil. Cook for 15 minutes, then drain and remove the inner skins (see page 95).

Return the skinned chestnuts to the pan and add the milk, the remaining sugar, vanilla and a pinch of salt. Cook over moderate heat for about 20 minutes or until all the milk is absorbed.

Remove the vanilla pod and press the chestnuts through a fine-meshed sieve or strainer. Let the little strands of chestnut purée land on the serving dish in the form of a mountain. Leave to cool.

Coat the mountain with the whipped cream, spreading from the top downwards. Dipping the spatula in cold water every so often is helpful. Keep chilled until serving. *Serves 6.*

Amaretto Pudding

BUDINO DI AMARETTO

1.4 kg/3lb pumpkin, peeled and
cut into chunks
1 litre/1¾ pints/1 US quart
milk
6 amaretto biscuits (cookies),
crumbled
Pinch of salt
60g/2oz/5 tbsp sugar
3 eggs (US large), separated
15g/½oz/1 tbsp butter
2 tbsp bread crumbs
6 almonds

Amaretto is a typical Italian flavouring. The inclusion of pumpkin gives the pudding an unusual touch.

Place the pumpkin and milk in a saucepan over low heat and cook gently until the pumpkin has absorbed all the milk, about 10 minutes. Add the amaretto biscuits, salt and sugar and mix with a wooden spoon (or use a food processor), blending the ingredients thoroughly into a purée. Place in a bowl.

Preheat the oven to 200°C/400°F/Gas 6.

One by one, add the egg yolks to the mixture.

Beat the egg whites until stiff, then gently fold into the mixture.

Grease a 1½ litre/2½ pint/6 cup mould with the butter and sprinkle with the bread crumbs. Arrange the almonds on the bottom of the mould. Pour in the pumpkin mixture. Bake for 45 minutes. Leave to cool before turning out. Serve chilled or at room temperature. *Serves 6.*

Rice Pudding with Raisins

DOLCE DI RISO E UVETTA SULTANINA

1 litre / 1¾ pints / 1 US quart
milk
150g / 5oz / ¾ cup sugar
45g / 1½oz / 3 tbsp butter
1 vanilla pod (vanilla bean)
Salt
240g / 8oz / 1½ cups short-grain
pudding rice
6 egg yolks
60g / 2oz / ⅓ cup raisins, soaked
in 5 tbsp Marsala, drained and
patted dry
Grated zest of 1 lemon
90g / 3oz / ¾ cup pecans, roughly
chopped

A delicious dessert, much loved by children, this can be eaten hot or cold.

Put the milk in a saucepan and bring to the boil. Add the sugar, butter, vanilla and a pinch of salt. Mix well. When the milk comes back to the boil add the rice. Cook gently for about half an hour. Drain if necessary and let cool.
Preheat the oven to 180°C / 350°F / Gas 4.
Transfer the rice to a bowl and remove the vanilla bean. Add the egg yolks, raisins, lemon zest and pecans. Mix well. Pour into a buttered baking dish, about 20 x 30cm / 8 x 12 inches. Bake for about 20 minutes or until the surface is golden. Serve hot or at room temperature. *Serves 6.*

Whole Wheat Ring Cake with Yogurt

CIAMBELLA INTEGRALE ALLO YOGHURT

150g / 5oz / 1¼ cups whole wheat
flour
30g / 1oz / 3 tbsp light brown
sugar
Pinch of salt
125ml / 4fl oz / ½ cup plain
yogurt
6 tbsp extra virgin olive oil
Grated zest of 2 lemons
3 eggs
15g / ½oz / 2 tsp baking powder
A few drops of vanilla essence
(vanilla extract)

This cake, light and only slightly sweet, makes perfect breakfast fare or children's snack, and is ideal when you have a sudden urge for a sweet treat yourself.

Preheat the oven to 180°C / 350°F / Gas 4.
Blend the flour, sugar, salt, yogurt, oil, lemon zest, 1 egg, the baking powder and vanilla essence together in a food processor. When these ingredients are well amalgamated, gradually add the remaining 2 eggs.
Grease a ring mould, 20cm / 8 inches in diameter, with butter. Sprinkle with whole wheat flour. Pour in the cake mixture. Bake for about 45 minutes. Test to see whether it is done by piercing the cake with a skewer. It is ready if the skewer comes out clean. Turn on to a wire rack and serve hot or cold.
Serves 6.

Lemon and Berry Cream

CREMA AL LIMONE E FRUTTI DI BOSCO

4 egg yolks
90g / 3oz / ½ cup caster sugar
(granulated sugar)
500ml / 16fl oz / 2 cups milk
Grated zest of 2 lemons
Juice of 1 lemon
400g / 14oz / 2 cups fresh berries
in season such as blueberries,
blackberries or raspberries

The most intriguing thing about this recipe is the contrast between the velvety texture of the cream and the tart and tangy flavour of the fresh berries.

Combine the egg yolks with the sugar in a heatproof bowl. Beat until light in colour. Heat the milk slightly, then add it with the lemon zest to the egg mixture. Set the bowl over a pan of gently simmering water (or use a double boiler). Heat the mixture very gently till creamy, stirring constantly. Do not boil.

Remove the bowl from the heat and add the lemon juice. Pour into 4 large shallow bowls and put a piece of dampened greaseproof paper (parchment paper) on the surface of each to prevent a skin from forming. Leave to cool. Sprinkle with the berries just before serving. *Serves 4.*

Castagnaccio

CASTAGNACCIO

240g / 8oz / 1⅔ cups chestnut
flour (available in specialty
shops)
2 tbsp extra virgin olive oil
Pinch of salt
4 tbsp water
90g / 3oz / ½ cup raisins, soaked
in warm water to soften,
drained and patted dry
120g / 4oz / 1⅓ cups pine nuts
1 tbsp chopped fresh rosemary
leaves

A very unusual blend of flavours is found in this traditional Tuscan speciality. Its sweetness, with a touch of rosemary, is irresistible.

Preheat the oven to 180°C / 350°F / Gas 4. Mix the chestnut flour with half the oil and the salt in a bowl. Add the water a little at a time, stirring well with a fork so no lumps form. The dough should not be too dense. Add the raisins, pine nuts and rosemary. Mix

well. (Alternatively use a food processor.) Grease a 28cm / 10 inch round cake pan with the remaining oil and place the dough in the pan. Bake for about 40 minutes or until solid and a light crust has formed. Leave to cool on a wire rack before serving. *Serves 4-6.*

Lemon and Berry Cream

Cats' Tongues

LINGUE DI GATTO

120g / 4oz / 1 stick (½ cup)
butter, at room temperature,
cut into pieces
Pinch of salt
120g / 4oz / ½ cup caster sugar
(granulated sugar)
120g / 4oz / ¾ cup plain flour
(all-purpose flour)
3 egg whites
1 tbsp almond oil (available in
specialty shops)
90g / 3oz plain (semisweet)
chocolate

Ideal for serving with Zabaione (page 157), these tasty little biscuits (cookies) are curved like cats' tongues. They can also be made chocolate-flavoured with the addition of 30g / 1oz / ⅓ cup unsweetened cocoa powder to the dough with the flour.

Place the butter, salt and sugar in a small bowl and beat with a wooden spoon until smooth and creamy. (You could also use a food processor or electric mixer.) Add the flour carefully so as not to form lumps. Beat the egg whites until stiff and fold gently into the mixture.
Preheat the oven to 240°C / 475°F / Gas 9.
Grease a baking sheet with butter and sprinkle with a little flour. Using a piping bag (pastry bag) with a wide smooth nozzle, pipe strips of the mixture about 6cm / 2½

inches long. Do not pipe them close together, to allow for spreading. Leave to sit for about 10 minutes.
Bake the biscuits (cookies) in 2 batches for 6-7 minutes until light golden. Grease a rolling pin with a little almond oil and drape each biscuit (cookie) over it to give it a light curve. Leave to cool.
Melt the chocolate in a double boiler or a bowl over a pan of simmering water. Using a brush, paint the inside of the curves. Leave to set before serving. *Makes about 30 biscuits.*

Fried Semolina Diamonds

DIAMANTI DI SEMOLINO FRITTI

375ml / 12fl oz / 1½ cups milk
2 tbsp honey
Pinch of salt
120g / 4oz / ⅔ cup semolina
(farina)
1 egg yolk
120g / 4oz / 1 stick (½ cup)
butter for frying
60g / 2oz / 1 cup fine bread
crumbs
A few tbsp caster sugar
(granulated sugar)

These are exquisite served with a fresh fruit dessert or with a fruit jam such as Plum and Cinnamon Jam (page 148).

Heat the milk with the honey and salt in a saucepan. As soon as it boils, add the semolina in a fine stream, stirring carefully so as not to form lumps. Cook over low heat for about 10 minutes, stirring constantly. Remove from the heat and mix in the egg yolk.
Dampen a baking sheet or shallow pan with a little cold water. Pour in the semolina mixture in a 2.5cm / 1 inch layer. Leave to cool.

Turn out, upside down, on to a working surface. Using a wet knife blade cut the semolina into diamond shapes, each measuring 6cm / 2½ inches in length.
Melt the butter in a large frying pan. Dip the diamonds in the bread crumbs and fry them until golden. Drain briefly on paper towels. Sprinkle with a little sugar, arrange on a heated serving dish and serve. *Serves 4.*

Chocolate Cake

TORTA DI CIOCCOLATO

450g / 1lb plain (semisweet)
chocolate, cut into little chunks
210g / 7oz / 14 tbsp butter, cut
into little pieces
2 tbsp caster sugar (granulated
sugar)
6 eggs
Pinch of ground cinnamon
250ml / 8fl oz / 1 cup whipping
cream (heavy cream)
Pinch of salt

This is the quintessential chocolate cake, rich and concentrated in flavour.
Serve it for anniversaries and other festive occasions. The secret is to use
top-quality chocolate.

Preheat the oven to 220°C / 425°F / Gas 7.
Melt the chocolate in a heatproof bowl over a saucepan of boiling water. Add the butter and 1 tbsp sugar and stir until smooth. Remove from the heat and keep warm.

Using a double boiler or a bowl set over a pan of simmering water, whisk the eggs with the cinnamon to body heat (36°C / 98°F). Remove from the heat. Whisk or beat until tripled in volume. Add half the egg mixture to the chocolate and mix well, then mix in the other half.

Grease a 26cm / 10½ inch round cake pan with a little butter and line the bottom with parchment paper. Pour in the cake mixture. Bake for 5 minutes, then cover with another sheet of parchment paper, greased with a little butter. Bake for a further 10 minutes. Remove from the oven and cool on a wire rack for 45 minutes. Refrigerate for 3 hours.

Turn out the cake, upside down, on to a serving dish. Let it sit for a while to return to room temperature.

Whip the cream with the salt and remaining sugar to stiff peaks. Transfer to a bowl and serve with the cake. *Serves 6-8.*

Oranges Filled with Fruit Salad

ARANCE RIPIENE DI MACEDONIA

2 large oranges
1 apple
Juice of ½ lemon
1 banana
3 tbsp sugar
Pinch of ground cinnamon
125ml / 4fl oz / 1 cup whipping
cream (heavy cream)

If you can, use oranges that have not been treated with wax and chemicals. If these are unobtainable, wash your oranges very well. An alternative to whipped cream would be to serve these with Tangerine Ice Cream (page 145).

Cut the oranges in half. Squeeze the juice, carefully scoop out and discard all their pulp. Reserve the juice. Peel the apple and cut into little cubes. Place in a bowl and sprinkle with the lemon juice. Cut the banana into slices and add to the apple. Add 2 tbsp sugar, the cinnamon and orange juice. Stir gently and chill for about an hour to let the flavours mingle. Fill the orange shells with the fruit salad and arrange them on a serving dish.

Whip the cream with the remaining sugar until stiff. Put it in a piping bag (pastry bag) and pipe decoratively on top of the oranges just before serving. Keep in the refrigerator until time for serving.
Serves 4.

Cherries in Wine Syrup

CILIEGIE IN SALSA DI VINO

900g / 2lb cherries
500ml / 16fl oz / 2 cups red wine
90g / 3oz / ½ cup caster sugar
(granulated sugar)
1 cinnamon stick

For this recipe choose a good-quality wine. This recipe also works very well with pears, scooped into little balls the size of cherries.

Remove the stems and pits from the cherries. Place them in a large saucepan. Add the wine, sugar and cinnamon stick, cover and simmer for about 10 minutes. Using a slotted spoon, remove the cherries and place in 4 small cups.
Leave to cool.
Continue boiling the syrup, uncovered, until it thickens. To check if the syrup is ready, dip in a spoon and blow on it to cool. When ready it will stick to the spoon.
Remove from heat, remove the cinnamon stick and cool to room temperature. Chill for a few hours.
Pour the syrup over the cherries and serve. *Serves 4.*

Moulded Lemon Jelly with Violets and Blackberries

GELATINA DI LIMONI ALLE MORE

750ml / 1¼ pints / 3 cups water
Grated zest and juice of 4 lemons
120g / 4oz / ⅔ cup caster sugar
(granulated sugar)
1½ tbsp powdered vegetarian gelatine
30g / 1oz / 1 tbsp violets, organically grown
300g / 10oz / 1⅔ cups blackberries

Beautiful and aromatic, this jellied mould would make a light finish to a very elegant lunch. There are many other edible flowers that could be used, including nasturtiums, orange blossoms and elderflowers (elderberry flowers). Some varieties of elderflower are poisonous, so do make sure you use the edible varieties.

Put the water, lemon zest and sugar in a saucepan to heat without boiling. Remove from the heat and leave to infuse for 15 minutes, then strain. While still hot, remove a small cupful and dissolve the gelatine in it. Mix with the lemon juice and return to the saucepan.
Dampen the inside of a 1 litre / 2 pint / 1 US quart mould with a little cold water. Arrange a little ring of violets at the bottom. Pour in enough of the liquid lemon jelly to cover them and chill in the refrigerator for about an hour or until set.
Add the remaining violets and enough liquid lemon jelly to half fill the mould. Replace in the refrigerator and chill for another hour or until this too is set.
Add the blackberries and the remaining liquid lemon jelly to fill the mould. Chill until completely set.
Run a knife blade around the inside rim. Dip the mould briefly in hot water, cover with a plate and turn upside-down to unmould. Serve immediately. *Serves 4.*

Ricotta and Pear Semifreddo with Thyme

SEMIFREDDO DI RICOTTA E PERE AL TIMO

3 pears, peeled and cored
1 tsp lemon juice
210g / 7oz / 1 cup ricotta cheese
4 tbsp honey
1 tsp ground cinnamon
2 tbsp rum
2 egg whites
Sprig of fresh thyme, leaves only

This is a very elegant and refreshing dessert, perfect for special occasions. Make sure the pears are tree-ripened for maximum flavour.

Blend the pears with the lemon juice in a food processor until smooth. Mix with the ricotta, honey, cinnamon and rum. Beat the egg whites until stiff and fold into the mixture. Divide among 4 freezerproof cups, sprinkle with thyme leaves and freeze for a couple of hours.
Serves 4.

Tangerine Ice Cream

GELATO AL MANDARINO

1 egg plus 1 yolk
90g / 3oz / ⅓ cup caster sugar (granulated sugar)
250ml / 8fl oz / 1 cup freshly squeezed tangerine juice
125ml / 4fl oz / ½ cup whipping cream (heavy cream)
Juice of 1 lemon
A few drops of vanilla essence (vanilla extract)

This ice cream is perfect for an elegant dinner. Apart from tangerines, clementines, satsumas and similar citrus fruit, you can also make it with orange juice, slightly increasing the amount of sugar. If you don't have an ice cream maker, freeze the mixture in a shallow pan until it is almost solid, then blend it in a food processor. Replace it in the freezer to finish the freezing.

Beat the egg, egg yolk and sugar until pale and creamy. Add the tangerine juice, cream, lemon juice and vanilla. Blend well together. Transfer the mixture to an ice cream maker and freeze.
Serves 4-6.

Overleaf: Tangerine Ice Cream, Ricotta and Pear Semifreddo with Thyme

Ice Cream

GELATO DI CREMA

5 egg yolks
210g / 7oz / 1 cup caster sugar
(granulated sugar)
1 litre / 1¾ pints / 1 US quart
double or whipping cream
(heavy cream)

Rich as it is irresistible, this dessert can be made successfully even without a machine. All you have to do is stir it a couple of times while it's freezing. This can be made with a top quality honey instead of sugar; warm the honey in a double boiler if it is very thick and set.

Beat together the egg yolks and sugar in a heatproof bowl until pale and creamy. Set the bowl over a saucepan of simmering water and add the cream, little by little, stirring constantly, or use a double boiler. Cook until thickened, stirring. Do not boil.

Leave to cool, then transfer to an ice cream maker to freeze. *Serves 8-10.*

Plum and Cinnamon Jam

MARMELLATA DI PRUGNE ALLA CANNELLA

450g / 1lb plums, washed and pitted
1 cinnamon stick
240g / 8oz / 1 cup plus 2 tbsp
caster sugar (granulated sugar)

Jams are a wonderful way to conserve the sunny flavours of summer for the cold seasons. There are so many excellent ones on the market that it's only really worth making jam if you have access to fresh fruit to harvest, in which case the jars make nice personal memories.

Preheat the oven to 150°C / 300°F / Gas 2.
Place the plums in a heavy-bottomed saucepan and cook them over low heat until soft.
Mix in the cinnamon and 60g / 2oz / 5 tbsp sugar. Transfer to a baking dish. Bake for about 40 minutes.

Add another 60g / 2oz / 5 tbsp sugar and mix. Bake for another 40 minutes. Repeat this process twice more till you run out of sugar.
Discard the cinnamon stick. Spoon into clean sterilized little jars and seal. Store in the refrigerator.
Makes about 450g / 1lb / 2cups.

Blackberry Jelly

GELATINA DI MORE

1.8 kg/4lb blackberries
Juice of 1 lemon
2 green apples, cut into pieces
(unpeeled)
1.5 kg/3lb 3oz/7½ cups caster
sugar (granulated sugar)

As beautiful to admire as it is to eat, this preserve is the best way to celebrate after a berry-picking walk in the mountains during blackberry season. You'll find it delicious on pancakes or crêpes or with Fried Semolina Diamonds (page 142).

Combine the blackberries with the lemon juice, apples and sugar in a large saucepan. Cook over low heat, stirring constantly and skimming the foam off the top often, until the jelly reaches setting point. Test by dipping in a spoon, putting a drop on a cold plate and tilting the plate. If the drop holds its shape, the jelly is ready.

Leave to drain through a jelly bag into a bowl. Pack the resulting jelly into sterilized jars, seal and keep in a cool dark place.
Makes about 450g/1lb/2 cups.

Chestnuts in Fennel Syrup

MARRONI AL FINOCCHIO

450g/1lb chestnuts
210g/7oz/1 cup caster sugar
(granulated sugar)
2 tbsp water
1 tbsp fennel seeds
Grated zest and juice of 1
lemon
1 vanilla pod (vanilla bean)

This combination of chestnuts and fennel seeds is typically Tuscan. You'll always have chestnuts ready for an emergency dessert, for example, for decorating a bowl of ice cream or simply served with whipped cream.

Remove the outer shells from the chestnuts. Make an incision in each one. Put the chestnuts in a saucepan and cover with water. Simmer for about 20 minutes or until they are tender. Leave the chestnuts in the water until they are cool enough to handle, then use a sharp knife to peel off the inner skin.

Meanwhile in a small saucepan, cook the sugar with the water, fennel seeds and lemon juice over low heat to make a syrup that sticks to a spoon.

Pack the chestnuts into a jar. Cover with the syrup and add the vanilla and lemon zest. Seal and sterilize by submerging in boiling water for 20 minutes. Let cool before removing from the water. Keep in a cool dark place.
Makes about 450g/1lb/2 cups.

breads, sauces AND *basic recipes*

This section offers a selection of the classic sauces that are used most frequently in Italian cuisine. They form an indispensable base for developing your skills. They can also serve as springboards to your imagination – with a little creative variation, substituting one herb for another for instance, you can invent all sorts of delicious alternatives.

For an Italian, sitting down at table without bread would be unthinkable. There will usually be several types in a small basket set in the middle of the table and bread will be eaten throughout the meal. Bread will even be served beside a plate of pasta, and it is a compliment to the chef to mop up the last exquisite drops of salad dressing, soup or sauce with a piece of bread. This great passion for bread in our culture has produced as many recipes as there are bakeries.

My memories are still vivid of the time when the wood oven was used to make bread in the purest Tuscan tradition – made into long loaves without any salt. This bread was stored on wooden shelves and remained delicious for several days. To this day bread is made without salt in Tuscany, and this bread's texture is particularly suited for the recipes of this area, such as *Panzanella* (Bread and Tomato Salad, page 111.)

Whole Wheat Bread with Nuts and Seeds

PANE INTEGRALE CON SEMI E NOCI

30g / 1oz fresh yeast
1 tsp sugar
350g / 12oz / 3 cups whole wheat flour plus more for kneading
2 tbsp extra virgin olive oil
Pinch of salt
250ml / 8fl oz / 1 cup warm water
2 tbsp roughly chopped walnuts
2 tbsp roughly chopped sunflower seeds
30g / 1oz / 3 tbsp raisins, soaked and patted dry
1 tbsp finely chopped fresh rosemary
Grated zest of 1 lemon
2 tbsp fennel seeds

This bread has a somewhat ambiguous character. Neither salty nor sweet, it makes a tasty accompaniment to cheese, especially the fresh moist varieties. It's also delicious with jams, honeys or other sweet spreads.

Mix the yeast and sugar with a little warm water. Make a little mountain of flour on a working surface and make a well in the middle. Pour in the oil, salt and water. Mix the ingredients with a fork, working from the centre, gradually incorporating the flour. When you can no longer use the fork, use your hands to knead into a smooth soft ball of dough. Brush away excess flour and continue to knead for a few minutes.

Sprinkle the inside of a bowl with flour, put in the dough and leave to rise in a warm place for about 20 minutes or until doubled in bulk.

Add the nuts, sunflower seeds, raisins, rosemary, lemon zest and fennel seeds to the dough and knead again well. Divide in half. Form each piece into a round shape and leave to rise again for half an hour.

Preheat the oven to 180°C / 350°F / Gas 4. Grease a baking sheet with butter, sprinkle with flour and arrange the loaves on it. Bake for 40 minutes. Allow to cool before slicing. *Makes 2 loaves.*

Carrot Bread

PANE DI CAROTE

450g / 1lb / 4 cups whole wheat flour
175ml / 6fl oz / ¾ cup milk
30g / 1oz fresh yeast
1 tsp sugar
1 tsp salt
60g / 2oz / 4 tbsp butter, melted
175ml / 6fl oz / ¾ cup carrot juice
210g / 7oz / 2 cups carrots, very finely grated

A lovely, colourful loaf which makes an unusual addition to the bread basket. It is delicious spread simply with a little butter, or used for sandwiches.

Make a mound of flour on a working surface and scoop out a good sized well in the centre. Warm the milk in a small saucepan and stir in the yeast and sugar with a fork. Pour into the well. Sprinkle the salt over the top and add the melted butter, carrot juice and grated carrots. Mix and knead all the ingredients together until you have a smooth soft ball of dough. Don't worry if the dough doesn't need all the flour. Transfer to a bowl. Cover and leave to rise in a warm place for about 20 minutes.

Knead again, then divide in half and shape into loaves. Put on a greased and floured baking sheet, or put into two greased and floured loaf pans. Leave to rise for a further 20 minutes.

Preheat the oven to 180°C / 350°F / Gas 4. Bake the loaves for 40 minutes. Allow to cool before slicing. *Makes 2 loaves.*

Rosemary Plaits (Braids)

TRECCE AL ROSMARINO

350g / 12oz / 3 cups whole wheat
flour, plus more for working
150g / 5oz / 1½ cups rye flour
30g / 1oz fresh yeast
1 tsp sugar
250ml / 8fl oz / 1 cup warm milk
60g / 2oz / 4 tbsp butter, melted
½ tsp salt
1 tsp chopped fresh rosemary
1 egg, beaten

Serve this very tasty bread with other rolls in a basket in the centre of the table. It makes an excellent accompaniment to a selection of cheeses at the end of a meal.

Make a little mountain of the two flours on a working surface and scoop out a well in the middle. Crumble the yeast into a small bowl, add the sugar and milk and mash well. Pour into the well together with the butter, salt and rosemary.

Begin mixing the ingredients with a fork, using a circular motion, then continue working with your hands until you have a smooth, elastic ball of dough. Don't try to force it to absorb more flour than it wants to. Transfer to a bowl and leave to rise in a warm place for about 25 minutes.

Knead a few more minutes, then divide into 6 equal portions. Shape them into ropes about 25cm / 10 inches long. Take three and make a plait (braid). Repeat with the remaining three.

Sprinkle a baking sheet with flour, arrange the loaves on it and brush with beaten egg. Leave to rise for 20 minutes.

Preheat the oven to 180°C / 350°F / Gas 4. Bake the bread for about 40 minutes.

Makes 2 plaits.

Potato Grissini with Sesame

GRISSINI DI PATATE AL SESAMO

210g / 7oz large potatoes
210g / 7oz / 1¾ cups whole wheat
flour, plus more for kneading
90g / 3oz / 6 tbsp butter
2 tbsp sesame seeds
1 tsp salt, plus more for
sprinkling

These grissini combine perfectly with little mouthfuls of mozzarella, or a creamy cheese such as ricotta.

Put a saucepan of water to boil. When boiling add the potatoes and cook for about 20 minutes or until tender. Drain, peel and mash them. Turn on to a working surface. Add the flour, butter, sesame seeds and salt. Knead together using your hands. You can also achieve the same result by working the potatoes (cut into pieces) with the other ingredients in a food processor.

Roll the dough into a fat sausage on the working surface. Cut slices about 1cm / ½ inch wide and, using your fingers, roll each slice into a thin snake about 20cm / 8 inches long. Sprinkle flour on the working surface every so often to stop it becoming sticky.

Preheat the oven to 170°C / 325°F / Gas 3.

Grease a baking sheet with butter. Lay out the grissini sticks, leaving a little space between each one. Sprinkle lightly with salt and bake for about 20 minutes or until they have turned golden.

Makes 8-10 grissini.

Rosemary Plaits

Béchamel Sauce

SALSA BESCIAMELLA

500ml / 16fl oz / 2 cups milk
30g / 1oz / 2 tbsp butter
30g / 1oz / 3 tbsp flour
Pinch of grated nutmeg
Salt

This velvety sauce is extraordinary in its ability to enrich a variety of dishes. It is wonderful with omelettes and potatoes. The version here is for pasta and foods that are particularly absorbent.

Heat the milk in a small saucepan without boiling. Keep warm.

Melt the butter in a saucepan over moderate heat and stir in the flour. Stirring constantly, cook until the mixture is lightly browned. Add the milk slowly in a thin stream, stirring. When all the milk has been absorbed, add the nutmeg and salt to taste and bring to the boil, stirring. Simmer until thickened.

Keep in a warm place, covered, so no skin forms on the surface.

A simple vegetable like cauliflower, barely half-cooked, may be arranged in a baking dish, covered with béchamel and popped into the oven for about 20 minutes, to become a delicious meal. This also holds true for many types of pasta – enriched with béchamel, tomato and a grating of Parmesan cheese and placed under the grill (broiler) to brown, it is transformed from something simple into something rich and elegant.
Serves 4.

Pesto

PESTO

60g / 2oz fresh basil leaves
30g / 1oz fresh mint leaves
60g / 2oz / ⅔ cup pine nuts
4 tbsp freshly grated Parmesan cheese
2 tbsp freshly grated pecorino cheese
125ml / 4fl oz / ½ cup extra virgin olive oil
Salt

Traditional Genovese pesto is a very ancient sauce. The little leaves of a particular variety of basil were pounded with a pestle and mortar and the other ingredients were added slowly so the result had a consistency almost as creamy as mayonnaise. Today we use a food processor, which is a lot simpler and yields excellent results. In this version I have enriched the pesto with mint leaves and omitted the garlic, necessary in the original version but a bit heavy.

Combine the basil, mint, pine nuts, Parmesan, pecorino, oil and a little salt in a blender or food processor. Blend till you have a dense sauce. Pesto keeps well in the refrigerator, provided you keep it covered with a thin layer of olive oil to prevent it oxidizing. It is a thick sauce; add stock or hot water to a few tablespoons of pesto to thin it for an accompaniment for steamed or boiled potatoes and sliced boiled meats. It can also be added to soups and rice in broth, potatoes and vegetable soups. *Serves 4-6.*

Tomato Sauce with Basil

SALSA DI POMODORO AL BASILICO

450g / 1lb ripe plum tomatoes
(or use canned)
90g / 3oz / 6 tbsp butter
1 small onion, chopped
1 tsp sugar
Salt
8-10 fresh basil leaves,
shredded by hand

A classic pillar of traditional Italian cooking, this sauce has two identities –
one, from the north, built around butter and onions, and the other,
from Florence in the south, based on extra virgin olive oil and garlic. The
buttery onion version blends better with egg pasta, such as fettuccine
and tagliatelle, and the garlicky one is ideal with dried pasta like spaghetti
and macaroni.

If fresh tomatoes are used, immerse in boiling water for half a minute, then drain and peel with a little knife. Cut in pieces and remove the seeds. If using canned tomatoes, drain and chop.

Melt the butter in a saucepan over low heat, add the onion and a couple of tablespoons of water and cover. Cook over moderate heat for about 10 minutes or until translucent, stirring occasionally. Add the tomatoes, sugar and salt to taste and continue cooking for about 20 minutes with the lid almost completely closed. Stir occasionally. Add water only if necessary: the sauce should be creamy and not too dry.

Stir in the basil, remove from the heat and let sit in a warm place until time for use.

When served with pasta it is customary to accompany this sauce with plenty of freshly grated Parmesan cheese. It can also be used with gnocchi, polenta, white rice, eggs and vegetables. It will keep in the refrigerator for a few days.

Serves 4.

Green Sauce

SALSA VERDE

60g / 2oz stale country-style
bread
4 tbsp chopped fresh flat-leaf
Italian parsley
1 hard-boiled egg, finely
chopped
2 tbsp chopped capers
Salt and pepper
125ml / 4fl oz / ½ cup extra
virgin olive oil
2 tbsp vinegar

This is a traditional North Italian sauce. It is very tasty and peps up steamed
or boiled vegetables like potatoes, carrots, courgettes (zucchini), turnips or
onions. It's also good on rice or as a dressing for tomato halves.

Soak the bread in a bowl of water for 10 minutes, then drain and squeeze dry.

Place the bread in a bowl with the parsley, egg and capers. Season to taste and add the oil and vinegar. Mix well. Transfer to a sauce boat and serve.

Green sauce will keep a few days in the refrigerator. *Serves 4.*

Soffritto with Oregano

SOFFRITTO ALL' ORIGANO

4 tbsp extra virgin olive oil
3 garlic cloves, chopped
1 small carrot, chopped
½ onion, chopped
1 bay leaf
1 celery stalk, chopped
½ cup dry white wine
Salt and pepper

Soffritto forms the basis for innumerable recipes. It is at the heart of the Mediterranean style of making tomato sauce, such as is found in the middle and south of Italy, and is perfect for dried pasta like spaghetti.
Soffritto adds flavour to all grains, pulses or legumes and vegetables. Your personal touch can come into play regarding your choice of herbs: oregano, basil, thyme and parsley are all felicitous.

The mark of a good cook is knowing how long to cook this sauce: it can be cooked for different lengths of time according to which recipe it will be used for. For instance, a minestrone would not need it very thoroughly cooked, whereas for a tomato sauce it adds a special character if you brown the vegetables first.
Heat the oil in a saucepan, add the garlic and fry for a few minutes over high heat. Add the carrot, onion, bay leaf and celery. Continue frying for 5 or 6 minutes over high heat, stirring often.
Pour in the white wine and continue cooking until it evaporates completely.
Lower the flame, season to taste, cover and continue cooking for anything between 15 and 30 minutes, stirring from time to time and adding a little water if necessary to keep the mixture moist, especially if you're cooking it for a longer period of time. Use it for sauces, soups, risotto, vegetables and so on. It keeps for a few days in the refrigerator. *Serves 4.*

Mayonnaise

SALSA MAIONESE

1 egg yolk (large)
Juice of ½ lemon
Salt and pepper
150ml / ¼ pint / ⅔ cup extra virgin olive oil

This is another case where the quality of the oil is absolutely crucial – it must be cold-pressed extra virgin olive oil. Mayonnaise is a very flexible condiment: it can be lightened with the addition of yogurt, or made richer with whipped cream. Used judiciously, the addition of garlic or herbs can give you a practically infinite variety of flavourings. It makes a great dressing for eggs, potatoes, tomatoes, cucumbers and all kinds of vegetables.

Combine the egg yolk, lemon juice, and a little salt and pepper in a food processor fitted with metal blades. Give a quick pulse to blend the ingredients. Leaving the motor running, add the oil in a thin stream until the mayonnaise thickens and becomes velvety.
Mayonnaise will keep in the refrigerator for a few days. *Serves 4.*

Vinaigrette

SALSA VINAIGRETTE

Pinch of salt
2 tbsp wine vinegar
4 tbsp extra virgin olive oil

This is one of the most traditional dressings for vegetables and salads. In daily Italian life one comes across it frequently in a side dish in one meal or another. Its studied simplicity serves to enhance the natural flavours of a salad, not cover them up.

It is vital that the ingredients be of excellent quality. Firstly, the oil should be extra virgin olive oil, mechanically not chemically extracted. Only oil pressed in this way retains the true flavour of the olives. Secondly, the vinegar must come from good wine and be produced by natural fermentation.

Dissolve the salt in the vinegar in a small bowl, stirring with a fork. Add the oil and combine well. *Serves 4.*

Zabaione

ZABAIONE

3 egg yolks
90g / 3oz / ½ cup caster sugar
(granulated sugar)
4 tbsp Marsala or Vinsanto
wine

Originally from Venice, Zabaione is very versatile. It can be mixed with crumbled amaretti biscuits (cookies) or mascarpone cheese as a delicious dessert or poured over berries, figs, cherries or stewed pears. It can also be used as a topping for tarts.

Combine the egg yolks and sugar in a heat-proof bowl. Beat with a whisk or portable (hand-held) electric mixer for a couple of minutes to dissolve the sugar completely. The mixture should lighten in colour.
Add the Marsala or Vinsanto, stirring well.
Set the bowl over a saucepan of simmering water or in a double boiler and continue to beat for about 4 minutes or until the mixture has doubled in volume. Transfer to a sauce boat or dessert glasses and serve immediately. Or keep in the refrigerator until needed.
Serves 4.

Vanilla Cream

CREMA DI VANIGLIA

250ml/8fl oz/1 cup milk
250ml/8fl oz/1 cup double
cream (heavy cream)
1 vanilla pod (vanilla bean)
2 egg yolks
60g/2oz/5 tbsp caster sugar
(granulated sugar)

Delicious hot or cold, this makes a perfect topping for ice cream, puddings, and stewed fruit such as prunes, pears, apples or berries. If you don't eat it right away, take care to stir it once in a while so the surface doesn't form a skin.

Warm the milk, cream and vanilla in a double boiler or a bowl set over a pan of simmering water.

Beat the egg yolks with the sugar until pale and creamy. Add a thin stream of the hot milk mixture, then pour back into the double boiler or bowl. Continue stirring as the cream thickens. Do not let it boil.

Remove the vanilla before serving.
Serves 4.

Wine Syrup

SALSA DI VINO

1 litre/1¾ pints/4 cups red
wine
450g/1lb/2¼ cups caster sugar
(granulated sugar)

Invented in an age when all left-over wine was found a use, this syrup is so good that it deserves to be made with top-quality wine, though it should not be one with too much body. This recipe works equally well either hot or cold. A superb topping for ice cream, it also marries well with stewed fruit, especially apples and pears, which are then transformed into an irresistible dessert. You can spice it up a bit by adding cinnamon or cloves.

Mix together the wine and sugar in a saucepan over medium heat. When the sugar has dissolved, simmer until it becomes syrupy. To check if the syrup is ready, dip in a spoon and blow on it to cool. When ready, it will stick to the spoon.

Leave to cool, then pour into sterilized glass containers.

Wine syrup keeps perfectly in the refrigerator, to be used whenever you need it.
Makes 450-600g/1-1¼lb/2-2¼ cups.

Index